D1125627

Caruso's 1920 Memento for his Coach and Accompanist

CARUSO
AND THE
ART OF SINGING

INCLUDING CARUSO'S VOCAL EXERCISES
AND HIS PRACTICAL ADVICE TO STUDENTS
AND TEACHERS OF SINGING

SALVATORE FUCITO
(Caruso's Coach and Accompanist, 1915–1921)
AND
BARNET J. BEYER

DOVER PUBLICATIONS, INC.
NEW YORK

Published in Canada by General Publishing Company, Ltd., 30 Lesmill Road, Don Mills, Toronto, Ontario.

Published in the United Kingdom by Constable and Company, Ltd., 3 The Lanchesters, 162–164 Fulham Palace Road, London W6 9ER.

Bibliographical Note

This Dover edition, first published in 1995, is an unabridged but reorganized republication of the work originally published by Frederick A. Stokes Company, New York, 1922. The Dover edition: corrects the original sequence of front matter; adds references, in the contents listing, to the subdivisions of Chapter VII and to the exercises in Chapter VI, VII and IX; adds a new list of reordered and repaginated illustrations (now grouped at the end of the text); and makes minor corrections in the text. Unnecessary part-title and blank pages have been deleted to improve the book's layout.

Library of Congress Cataloging-in-Publication Data

Fucito, Salvatore.
    Caruso and the art of singing : including Caruso's vocal exercises and his practical advice to students and teachers of singing : with ten portraits and five caricatures / by Salvatore Fucito and Barnet J. Beyer.
        p.   cm.
    Originally published: New York : F. A. Stokes, ©1922. With rev. front matter and minor corrections to the text.
    ISBN 0-486-28456-5
    1. Caruso, Enrico, 1873–1921. 2. Singing. 3. Singing—Studies and exercises. I. Beyer, Barnet J. (Barnet Julius), 1887–1947. II. Title.
ML420.C259F9   1995
783—dc20
                                     94-23634
                                         CIP
                                       MN

Manufactured in the United States of America
Dover Publications, Inc., 31 East 2nd Street, Mineola, N.Y. 11501

CONTENTS

LIST OF ILLUSTRATIONS

PREFACE

I FEEL that it was the greatest honor of my life when, in 1915, my distinguished friend Enrico Caruso called me to New York to be his coach and accompanist. I had previously served him in the same capacities during his frequent visits to Berlin, where our closer friendship began in the year of 1909. In those days I always eagerly awaited Caruso's arrival in Berlin, not only because it was an inspiration and a musical education to work with the great master of song, but also because his very presence diffused sunshine and happiness. In fact, it is difficult for me to say whom I loved more, Caruso the artist or Caruso the man—both were so great.

During the years that I spent with Caruso he often talked to me about his life, his struggles, and his triumphs, as well as about his art. He always spoke very modestly of his phenomenal achievement, but he loved his art and often discussed its vexing problems.

For he was much more than a magical voice: he was consciously an artist, an artist whose extraordinary vocal and dramatic powers were in great measure the fruits of a thorough comprehension of his art. Whenever he wished to produce an effect, he could contrive a means to accomplish it. He devised exercises—which are included in the book—that reveal a remarkable insight into what is required to make the singing voice agile and flexible. And the vowels he employed to blend and color his tones demonstrate that even his tone mastery was conditioned by his directing intelligence.

Two considerations have prompted me to write this book on Enrico Caruso's art: first, the desire to pay my tribute to the memory of a friend and a great artist; and, second, the hope that I could pass on to all who are concerned with the art of singing Caruso's methods in breathing and producing tones, his vocal exercises and his views on vocal technique, his ideals of singing as well as his practical advice to singers. I have dwelt on his life only in so far as it was closely related to his art, and I have essayed to set down some of the recollections he was so fond of telling. Whenever I have quoted Caruso, I have endeavored to recall as nearly as possible the exact words he used. S. F.

CARUSO
AND THE
ART OF SINGING

CHAPTER I

CARUSO'S BOYHOOD AND EARLY TRAINING

"ENRICO CARUSO is dead. The enormous displacement caused by this lamentable happening is not alone confined to the artistic sphere but literally to the entire civilized world. We doubt if there are more than a half dozen public men on the globe to-day whose demise would so stir the universal imagination as has the passing of the incomparable tenor. . . ." So wrote the late James Gibbons Huneker, and the entire press of the country, nay, of the world, voiced the same feeling of grief and veneration.

Caruso had won the hearts of thousands of people in all walks of life. We know of no death in the annals of song that roused so much attention and shocked so many people

2

as when Caruso breathed his last. In many lands his heroic struggle to stay death was followed with great anxiety, and when the news was flashed the world over that Caruso had finally succumbed, that he was no more, a wave of deep sorrow swept the myriads who loved and admired him. There were two countries where the great loss was perhaps felt more than elsewhere: in Italy, his native land, to which he remained loyal and where he was worshipped; and in America, his adopted country, where he was loved as a native son.

The story of Enrico Caruso's life is that of his art: the two are inseparable. The private fortunes and the public career of one of the greatest singers of all time, and the greatest tenor of his day, are so closely interwoven that to all intents and purposes they are one. His life was song, and song was his life. And yet, unlike many singers, Caruso was deeply interested in many provinces of art and culture quite beyond the boundaries of music. He has so often been misrepresented as an artist whose intellectual attainment was completely overshadowed by a phenomenal voice, that one who knew him as intimately as did the writer cannot insist too strongly upon the variety and breadth of his knowledge, his keen insight, his great activity, his powers of observation and of memory. A mere phenomenal voice could not have held that unique place among singing men. Any man who, with an art such as Caruso's, can so intensely move musicians and laymen alike is more than the fortunate possessor of a wonderful vocal instrument. Caruso's intelligence and personality played no small part in the achievements of a career crowned with the laurel of world-wide admiration and reverence.

Enrico Caruso was born February 27, 1873, in Naples, that city of blue skies and glowing sunlight which contests with Constantinople the claim of occupying the most beautiful site in Europe. Marcellino Caruso, his father, was a skilled mechanic of an inventive turn of mind who was employed in the Meuricoffre importing establishment. He and his wife, Anna, lived in the thickly populated working-class quarter which surrounds the railroad station where the tourist takes the train for Pompeii. Little Enrico, one of a family of three children, was a happy-go-lucky boy, full of sun and mischief.   He took to the water almost as soon as he was able to walk, and up to the age of ten haunted the warehouse docks of Naples, swimming for hours with other youngsters of his own age and indulging in those day-dreams of running away from home and becoming a sailor which are common to all children in a seaport city.   When he reached his tenth year, his father told him that he would either have to learn a trade or go to school, and Enrico accepted the latter alternative as the lesser of two evils.   But his school life was a stormy one.   The boy was unused to restraint, and it was quite natural that he should play truant, and find his way back to the semi-aquatic life of the waterfront which he loved so well.   Having learned the art of self-defense in the strenuous school of the docks, he was well able to take care of himself when difficulties arose between his fellow-pupils and himself, and he was often in trouble because of his readiness to accept a challenge.   He was noisy and lively, and earned many a whipping at home for neglecting his lessons and getting into scrapes that grew out of his boyish mischievousness.

Every youngster in Naples fancies himself a singer; but even at this early age it was evident that Enrico had a voice out of the ordinary. It attracted the attention of the headmaster of the school which he attended. Himself a musician, this teacher drilled Enrico privately and developed his fine boy contralto, coaxing him to learn by gifts of candy and exemptions from school work. He then proceeded to exploit the voice he had trained by securing engagements for Enrico to sing at fashionable weddings and concerts—and pocketing the proceeds of his appearances.

But Enrico's schooling was not destined to be of long duration. By the time he was twelve years old the boy had made school so unhappily eventful for his teachers that he was sent home in disgrace. His father, deciding that further educational efforts would prove to be love's labor lost, first gave him a severe thrashing, and then entered him as a draftsman's apprentice in the De Lucca Mechanical Laboratories. Mechanical engineering is no profession for an artist, and Enrico did not take to it. He did not rebel openly, since his mother, to whom he was devotedly attached, wished him to learn something practical; but he heartily disliked his work, and could interest himself in but a single phase of it—mechanical drawing. And even his mechanical drawing he regarded purely as a stepping-stone to higher artistic ambitions, for by now he had made up his mind to become an artist. His love for drawing and for caricature—he drew more caricatures than designs—dates from this time. When Enrico was fifteen years of age his mother died; and now that her wishes, which alone had induced him to continue at work he loathed, no longer bound him, he declared that he was through with mechanical engineering forever.

His declaration of independence had results. His father, strangely enough in the case of an Italian, was entirely unmusical, and was fixed in his resolve that his son should learn some trade or profession of practical and utilitarian value; he had no sympathy with what he regarded as Enrico's extravagant and hairbrained ideas. He himself was a mechanic, and as a mechanic he had done well. Let his son follow in the paternal footsteps. But this was what Enrico was temperamentally unable to do.   When he told his father that he had come to an unalterable decision to devote himself entirely to art and to music, the older Caruso informed him in a rage that he could take his choice of starving or becoming a mechanic; and when the boy obstinately refused to have anything more to do with engineering in any way, shape, or form, his father called him a disgrace to the family and ordered him out of the house.

Enrico did not hesitate to take his father at his word.   He was only fifteen, but he was already filled with that optimistic courage, which throughout his life deserted him only on the rarest occasions, that courage which he so strikingly displayed during his last illness in New York.   If he was to become a singer, the sooner he began the better.   Turning his back on the home which had been denied him, he became a *scugnizzo,* a Gavroche of the Neapolitan streets, singing for a few *soldi* or for the pure joy of song, wherever and whenever opportunity offered.   Known as "Arrichetiello," he was occasionally allowed to sing gratuitously in one or two of the tiny theaters near the old Piazza Castello, and then, after a time, regularly, for a small recompense, in a sailors' café-concert near the Mole and the Immacolatella Vecchia, the old port of the days of the Bourbon kings, in which at that time the whole maritime life of the city was concentrated. He also sang—for one *lira,* twenty cents—at the long Tuesday services of the Church of Sant' Anna alle Paludi. His other assets, aside from his voice, were his unconquerable optimism and his splendid physique, although the former did not always prevent his going to bed hungry. During this early period of stress and struggle, the fifteen-year-old boy who would be an artist was at times forced to seek other, less congenial work, merely to keep body and soul together. Thus, on one occasion, he managed to obtain a position as outrider in the stables of the Count of Bari, a position which his size and weight fortunately prevented his holding for any length of time.

Yet he was gradually becoming known as the best boy singer in the city of Naples. He had made no more than a precarious living singing in the cafés and hostelries of the waterfront. Now his increasing reputation secured him more frequent and better paid engagements in private houses and at church festivals. His voice, too, assumed a wonderful quality, and this merely led to his being more than ever in demand.

Once, rumor has it, when he sang in one of the Neapolitan churches, the then Prince of Wales, later King Edward VII, happened to be present, and was so impressed with his voice and his singing that he had conveyed to him an offer to go to England on liberal terms, an offer of which Enrico did not take advantage. For about two years the boy managed to sing his way through life in this manner, and had progressed from what was literally a hand-to-mouth existence to a position of relative comfort, with money flowing in plentifully when—his voice broke!

No matter what its beauty or quality, the boy voice is but a fleeting possession. Nature has fixed its term within limits which vary but little, and it is not until the vocal transition which marks the change to puberty has taken place, that the singing voice develops under new conditions. Enrico had given hardly a thought to the evanescent character of that clear and crystalline boy voice which had made him a favorite in a small way. Suddenly he was deprived of it. When he attempted to sing he could produce only the shrill, rough, whistling sounds which feature the transition period.

It is no wonder that the optimistic young boy, who at last had really begun to believe himself justified in choosing music for a career, even though he had been turned out of doors for so doing, was dumbfounded. The breaking of his voice seemed to him a veritable catastrophe, one beyond repair. Here he was, the idol of the frequenters of the Caffè del Molo—where the Piedigrotta songs came into being—and accounted the best singer in the churches of his home city, and quite suddenly he found himself voiceless. The abrupt interruption of all his activities made him feel almost that his voice had left him forever and fear that now his hopes and ambitions would never be realized.

It was his second great sorrow. He shut himself up in despair, and would see none of his many friends. But a youth of Enrico's happy disposition could not despair forever.

It was in the summer, and one day he was tempted from his retirement by some comrades who wanted him to go swimming with them. He forgot his voice and joined them, and on their way to the water, he even sang, sang and croaked as well as he could, and for the moment thought no more of it, one way or another.

On his way home, however, he chanced to enter into conversation with Edoardo Missiano, a young fellow who was a good amateur baritone and the son of a wealthy family of Naples. Missiano, who had heard Enrico sing at the Bagni del Risorgimento, told him that he had a genuine tenor voice, and offered to take him to his lodgings and try it out. Enrico, whose unhappiness over what had seemed to be the loss of his vocal powers had driven him to contemplate suicide, now felt the resurgence of all those doubts and despairs which for a short time he had escaped. He tried to evade Missiano's offer, but the latter insisted so vigorously that Enrico had, perforce, to accompany him to his rooms.

Missiano at once seated himself at the piano and struck a chord. "Sing!" he cried to

Caruso. Despairingly the youth attempted a note, but the sound he produced was so shrill and feeble that he said, almost in tears, "I can't do it! It has gone!" Missiano, however, persevered, and having made Caruso sing the scale, up and down, a few times, convinced himself that not only did the boy have a voice, but that his voice was one of unusual quality.

In his joy at his discovery he leaped from the piano-stool and lifted the despairing singer high in the air. "You fool, you idiot!" he cried. Enrico, thinking that Missiano was mocking him, felt his despair turn to rage. He took up a heavy brass candlestick standing near him, and hurled it at the young baritone with all his strength. "You are mad . . . " called the latter, as the missile crashed into a large mirror and wrecked it. "You are mad to think that your voice is gone! It is wonderful, and if you cultivate it you will be the first tenor of the century."

If Caruso's self-confidence and his belief in his voice had not been restored at this juncture, would he have abandoned his plans for an operatic career? It is possible, and yet it hardly seems probable. It is to Missiano, at any rate, that the discovery of Caruso's voice in the first instance is really due. Like Napoleon, the tenor was not one to forget those who had been kind to him before he came into his heritage of fame. In 1906, when Caruso visited Naples, he learned that Missiano, whose family had once been so well-to-do, had fallen upon evil days and was suffering actual poverty, and his influence was successfully exerted to secure a place for the baritone at the Metropolitan, where he was entrusted with minor parts.

Missiano lost no time in bringing Enrico to Guglielmo Vergine, a celebrated Italian vocal master, famed as the teacher of Antonio Scotti, of the tenor Bai, surnamed "the little Caruso," of Amelia Karola, Bai's wife—these two for a time rivaled the two Terrazzinis—of Pandolfini, Bellincioni, Russ, and other noted lyric artists who had had the benefit of his subtle disciplinary methods, based on the best traditions of the old Italian masters.

Vergine, however, did not seem particularly impressed with Caruso's voice at a first hearing. "It is like the gold at the bottom of the

Tiber," he said, "hardly worth drawing out." Missiano was not discouraged; he made Vergine promise to hear his protégé again, after an interval of five days, and then employed the intervening time in showing Caruso his worst defects and assiduously coaching him in certain arias which seemed calculated to show his voice to the best advantage, in so far as its quality and character were concerned, for it was evident that concerning interpretation and nuance he had much to learn.

When Enrico returned to Vergine he sang the "Siciliana" from Mascagni's "Cavalleria Rusticana," then at the height of its popularity, and the aria from Bizet's "I Pescatori di Perle" for the famous teacher, who, though still anything but enthusiastic regarding the tenor's future prospects, declared himself willing to accept him as a pupil and to do what he could to make an opera singer out of him.

Did a teacher of such reputation, whose pupils almost invariably made names for themselves, agree to train Caruso blindly, on a chance of his succeeding? Caruso himself is authority for the statement that Vergine, when first he heard him, regarded the Caruso throat as an indifferent one. Yet the contract which he insisted on Caruso's signing, a contract which guaranteed that Vergine should receive twenty-five per cent of all his pupil's earnings during his first five years in opera, though it may have been a pure speculation, appears to have been a very definite expression of confidence in the actual financial possibilities of Caruso's voice, once it had been placed, faceted, and polished by training.

That Vergine praised Caruso but little, and never gave him much encouragement while Caruso was studying with him, may have had its reasons. Enrico was at that time no more than an optimistic boy, easily satisfied and pleased with what he did. Vergine, with his contract in mind, would naturally try to make him concentrate intensively on his work, and to that end would not wish him to think so well of himself as to relax in his efforts.

Enrico took the best possible care of himself and worked hard, mentally and vocally, at the exercises prescribed for him. His progress was rapid, and he had already begun to look forward to the time when he might hope to make his operatic début, when his studies were abruptly interrupted.

The universal military service law, strictly enforced in Italy as in all other Continental countries, compelled the budding tenor to give up his solfeggi for soldiering. He made no attempt to evade the call of duty, promptly entered the army barracks, and was enrolled in the Thirteenth Regiment of Artillery, then in garrison at Rieti, in Perugia, a picturesque medieval town in the midst of a vine- and olive-growing countryside whose fertility was celebrated by both Virgil and Cicero.

In Rieti Enrico was a happy soldier, and soon became a favorite with his fellow artillery-men. When one of his comrades was sent to the guard-house for some slight offense, Enrico would ransom him by offering to sing for the officer of the day any song the latter especially wanted to hear. His offer was seldom refused, and as a result Enrico's company held him in high esteem. But so flagrant a laxity on the part of officers on duty, and so open a violation of regulations, was not to continue unchecked.

It was on a lovely Easter Day, all sunshine

and blue skies, that the storm broke which
suddenly ended Enrico's rôle as the savior of
delinquent cannoniers. The officers had given
a banquet to the soldiers of the regiment,
Major Nagliati, the commander, occupying
the place of honor at the head of the table. At
the conclusion of the dinner it was proposed,
and unanimously seconded, that in the Major's honor Enrico should sing the "Brindisi"
from "Cavalleria Rusticana." Enthusiastic
bravos and demands for an encore greeted the
conclusion of the song. It was then that
Major Nagliati raised his hand for silence and
made a little speech, short and very much to
the point, which put an effectual damper on
the festive spirit of the occasion. The Major
raked the regiment fore and aft, and Caruso
in particular, dwelling on the impropriety of
his putting that voice at every one's beck and
call, his unseemly use of it to effect the release
of military prisoners from the guard-house,
and the company's criminal folly in requesting
a singer to sing immediately after a meal.
Addressing himself to Enrico in particular,
he called him a fool, and said that Caruso was
unworthy of the great gift he evidently held

in such light esteem. In conclusion he declared that if any of the officers of his regiment again compelled Caruso to sing, he would have them put in irons, regardless of rank, and would have the singer punished as well.

Yet, on the other hand, it was this same Major Nagliati, who coming across the young recruit one morning, as he sat before the barracks polishing the brass buttons of his service uniform coat and singing "open-throated," from sheer joy of living, asked him what he did in civilian life. "I hope to become an opera singer," mumbled the abashed private, who could not imagine why the Major wanted to know. That very evening he was informed that the Major had hunted up a singing teacher for him, a talented amateur musician of Rieti. For the remainder of his two months' stay in the garrison town—for Caruso's army life only lasted some sixty days in all—he continued his interrupted studies under this tuition. His release from military service came about in a perfectly natural way. His father had remarried, and Enrico's stepmother, who had heard him sing and who realized the possibilities of his voice, urged the father to secure an honorable discharge. Enrico's father had not grown a whit more musical, but he had been much impressed by his son's progress and the favorable predictions made with regard to his future. The discharge was easily effected, thanks to his younger brother's willingness to serve out the rest of Enrico's time as a substitute.

After this short military interlude, Enrico returned to Vergine, and continued to study with him for another six months. He had studied with him some three years in all, when his teacher dismissed him with a soberly phrased letter of recommendation, and the young tenor began to cast about for operatic engagements.

Chapter II

CARUSO'S UPWARD CLIMB

In Italy, where tenor voices of lyric sweetness are to be found in profusion, young knights of the high C do not, as a rule, have an easy time of it. Many a singer is tolerated and even encouraged on French and German operatic stages, both small and large, who would be hissed off the boards in Italy. Caruso, however, did not fail to secure engagements, though none of his earlier appearances gave any indication of the fame to which he was to attain later.

He made his début in the Teatro Nuovo in Naples, where he appeared four times in the title-rôle of an unimportant opera, "L'Amico Francesco," by Morelli. Enrico received ten lire for each performance, with a pair of stage shoes, a suit of fleshings, and a neckerchief "thrown in." Twenty-six years later the artist who had been glad to accept a fee of ten lire for his first performance in grand opera, refused the $12,000 a performance of-

fered him for a series of appearances in Lima,
Peru. In Morelli's opera Caruso made no
very definite impression, one way or another.
The general opinion was that his voice had
a sympathetic quality of tone, but that it
was rather small and lacking in volume.
This opinion may have been more or less a result of Caruso's following Vergine's instructions to sing with restraint and not to let out
his voice, for Vergine's theories insisted that
the *forte* was the bane of the operatic voice
and that stress would kill it.

At any rate, his negative virtues sufficed to
secure him another opportunity. He was
engaged for the opera at Caserta, in Cam-
pania, a garrison town about twenty-one miles
from Naples. In Caserta he sang Turiddu,
Camoëns and—some prefer to consider this his
real début—Faust in Boito's "Mefistofele."
This was in April, 1895, and again Caruso
was paid at the rate of ten lire a night, or
about two dollars. But in Caserta his singing attracted more favorable attention; for,
much to Vergine's disgust, he abandoned his
maestro's advice and "let out" his voice.

In the following year fortune treated him

somewhat more kindly. He appeared at Genoa in "Traviata" and "Trovatore," and in "Traviata," "Favorita," and "Gioconda" in the Teatro Fondo at Naples, and in both cities with some measure of success. These were, perhaps, the first steps toward an increasing recognition of his artistic merits.

His engagement at the Fondo in Naples was followed in the same year by one at Salerno, in whose opera house the season was to be opened with a performance of Bellini's "I Puritani." Lombardi, the famous singing teacher, who was the conductor and who had heard favorable reports regarding Caruso, suggested his name to the management when his leading tenor fell ill at the eleventh hour. Caruso's earlier quasi-failures in Naples, whether or not due to the vocal suppression advocated by Vergine, had led to his being called "the broken tenor;" but although one of the directors of the Salerno opera mentioned this fact to Lombardi, the latter did not allow it to influence him. He sent for the young tenor, offered him the engagement, and found himself entirely justified by the manner in which Caruso acquitted himself of his

rôle. Caruso's operatic "market value" was
on the increase, and he himself was gaining
greater confidence in his vocal powers, as well
as greater artistic maturity in his interpretations.

Lombardi, who gave him much disinterested
advice during this engagement, induced him
to ignore Vergine's instructions to hold back
his voice and not let it out in all its sonorous
strength. He encouraged Caruso to cultivate
a vigorous attack and a robust style of vocalization, and told him that when he confronted
an audience he should carry himself like a
toreador, braving the natural skepticism of his
auditors with a veritable onslaught of tone.
The memory of this advice probably had its
share in developing that splendid vocal vigor
with which Caruso flung himself into his later
parts. There can be no doubt but that Lombardi had a most salutary influence on the
tenor. Vergine had cramped and bound his
voice. As the tenor himself declared: "He
restrained all my inclination to color a note,
deprived me of all power of emphasis. For
three years I studied against my grain, repres-

sing nature in order to become a Vergine product."

It was Lombardi who made clear to Caruso that he need not assume a cold and statuesque pose on the stage, singing his notes prettily without distinguishing among them with regard to intensity and color. As a precious outcome of his Salerno season under Lombardi, Caruso was able to say: "A great light shone upon me, and never again did I sing against nature. Thereafter I always sang with all the voice I had when the right moment came, and always with the color that my heart told me should envelop my poet's words. From that night when I sang "I Puritani" in Salerno, I was never again called 'the broken tenor.' "

Other engagements followed, in various Italian cities, and Vergine—not for Caruso's sake alone, as will appear—urged him to miss no opportunity to sing in public and make himself better known. This constant encouragement of Vergine's, his insistence that Caruso sing as often as possible, had a very genuine, a financial, motive. Whenever and wherever Caruso sang, his former teacher promptly put in an appearance to claim the twenty-five per cent of the tenor's receipts guaranteed him by his contract. Caruso never made any objection, but the monotonous regularity with which Vergine presented himself at the tenor's performances was so noticeable that it attracted the attention of one manager. He made some inquiries of Caruso; and when the tenor showed him the contract, he pointed out that, according to its terms, Vergine would be entitled to a quarter of all Caruso could earn during *five years of actual singing!* In other words, Caruso would be obliged to sing steadily until he reached the age of fifty before Vergine would have received his final payment. This discovery led Caruso to discuss with Vergine the unfair terms of the contract, and it is pleasant to know that when the matter was eventually referred to the Italian courts for settlement, Caruso was upheld and Vergine lost 200,000 lire by a decision rendered in the tenor's favor.

His first real outstanding success Caruso scored in the rôle of Marcello, in Leoncavallo's opera "Bohême," at the Teatro Lirico in Milan. He had already, in Livorno, sung Rodolfo in Puccini's more popular opera of the same name. On that occasion he had told Puccini that he could not put in the high C in the Romanza, and the latter had intimated that most tenors killed the aria for the sake of the high note, and that he would rather have the process reversed. Now Sonzogno, the Italian publisher of Leoncavallo's work, had brought him the latter's score, begging him to examine it, as he felt sure that it was admirably suited to the tenor's voice. Caruso, after studying it for some days with Vergine—this was before their difference, of course—convinced himself that he could not do justice to the part and would fail in it. Sonzogno, however, to whom he had returned the score, renewed the attack, and his entire faith that Caruso's success would be great and immediate so encouraged the tenor that he threw himself heart and soul into the preparation of the rôle. He sang it before a large audience on November 8, 1898, in the Lirico, and awakened the following morning to find that he had become famous.

The press and public united in agreeing that Caruso had not mistaken his vocation;

and this, his first success, was the real beginning of his artistic career. Among those who had heard him for the first time was Jules Massenet, whose "Navarraise" he. also sang during the same season. In his "Memoires" Massenet says: "Among my memories of Milan I have kept the recollection of being present at Caruso's début. The now famous tenor was very modest then, and when, a year later, I saw him wrapped in an ample fur coat, it was obvious that the figure of his salary must have mounted crescendo. When I saw him I did not envy him his brilliant fortune or his undoubted talent, but I did regret—that winter especially—that I could not put his rich, warm coat on my own back."

The impression Caruso had made on November eighth was intensified by his appearance at the Lirico on the sixteenth as the creator of the rôle of Loris at the première of Giordano's "Fedora." It was a part whose exuberant melodic character and dramatic effect the young artist improved to the utmost, and after his singing of Loris' confession of love, the short Giordano aria "Amor ti vieta di non amar," he was given a tremendous ovation, and was called before the curtain four times. The following morning all the critics agreed that Caruso had sung "Fedora"— *e la Fé 'd 'oro*—in a manner truly golden.

His position as an operatic tenor was now assured, though all his triumphs still lay before him. He sang in one Italian city after another, including Livorno and Genoa, where he was heard in Bizet's "I Pescatori di Perle" at the Carlo Felice. In fact, the Milan appearances of 1898 mark a distinct milestone in his development. The impression he made in them was instrumental in bringing about his transformation from a purely Italian singer into the great world artist, and in releasing him from the narrower sphere of the Italian operatic stage. An intelligent impresario, looking for a new voice which might justify an international career, decided he had found one in Caruso. As will be shown, his confidence was not misplaced.

Before we take up the second period of Caruso's career, his development as an operatic tenor of international fame, some considerations anent the natural and artistic means which aided him in his achievement may not be amiss. That Caruso was endowed with a remarkable physique, with a powerful pair of bellows, and with a wonderful vocal apparatus is common knowledge. Many physicians, competent and incompetent alike, have discoursed at length upon Caruso's marvelous vocal organism. Yet, after all, comparatively little is known about the precise workings of the little reed-like membranes which are called the vocal cords, or of the other adjacent vocal organs.

What we do know is that Caruso's natural advantages alone could never have made him the great artist he developed into. The physiologists have, as a rule, overlooked an all-important factor in the art of song—the mental factor. The voice of Caruso, light and lyric in quality at the beginning, prevented from coming into its own by Vergine's theories of repression, even in its later golden purity and dramatic poignancy owed those subtler inflections which move the human heart—the flawless, sustained legato, the exquisite mezza voce, the beautiful phrasing and expressive declamation—to the great tenor's unremitting hard work, both mental and technical, and to his fidelity to the ideals of interpretation which he never abandoned throughout his career. His great natural gift of an exceptional voice was always the interpreting medium for a controlling artistic mind, and his apparently effortless singing was not—as so many erroneously believe—a freak of nature, but the result of constant intensive devotion to the study, not only of his rôles, but also of the vocal exercises upon which his marvelous technique was based. Some of his own statements show how convinced he was that the most wonderful voice in the world is soulless unless it be spiritualized by the intellectual and emotional factors.

It was this firm conviction that counted heavily in Caruso's progress as a vocal artist; it was a doctrine which gave his art a solid foundation to build upon. Caruso fully comprehended the secret that to learn to sing beautifully is an endless task.

With this secret, and with what is now acknowledged to have been authentically the greatest natural tenor voice of the period ready to be revealed; backed by tireless, conscientious study; and equipped with a large repertory of tenor rôles; with youth, enthusiasm, and ideals to lend wings to his ambition, Enrico Caruso was indeed superbly prepared to embark on his stupendous international career in opera.

Chapter III

THE CONQUEST OF THE OLD WORLD

Caruso's first operatic flights beyond the limits of his native land did not take him immediately to the musically more famous capitals of Europe. The enhanced reputation which had prompted his engagement to create the tenor rôle in the first Italian production of Massenet's "Sapho," at the Scala in Milan, led to a short Egyptian excursion, though his successes in Cairo and Alexandria may be regarded as mere extensions of his Italian successes, since, musically speaking, Egypt is still as much a Roman colony as in the days of the emperors.

More important in spreading his rising fame abroad were two winter tours to Russia, where he made a great impression in Moscow and Petrograd, and the first of five successive summer seasons in Buenos Aires (1899-1903), which served to make him known in South America. In the fall of 1899 he appeared in the Costanzi in Rome and at the Communale in Bologna. It was in the latter theater that he first sang the rôle of Rhadames in "Aïda," and established his confidence in his high C, which hitherto he had regarded with a trace of distrust.

In 1900 he sang in Covent Garden, London, for the first time, appearing as Des Grieux in Puccini's "Manon Lescaut," his beautiful voice winning frenetic applause from the audience. The same year, at the Milan Scala, then directed by Gatti-Casazza and Toscanini, he opened the season triumphantly with Puccini's "La Bohème"; and in 1901, during the Carnival, he sang again in the same house, creating the Florindo of Mascagni's "Le Maschere." This opera, despite the fact that it was produced simultaneously at seven of the most important Italian opera houses—Rome, Milan, Turin, Genoa, Venice, Verona, and Naples—on January 17 of that year, was a failure, though Caruso did much to redeem the work by his convincing presentation of his part. He also appeared in Boito's "Mefistofele," and in Donizetti's "L'Elisir d'Amore"; and notwithstanding that two older tenors of established fame were still active on the operatic stage of his native land, Caruso had by this time been generally recognized by press and public as the foremost of Italian tenors.

In the autumn of 1901 he sang at Treviso and at Bologna in "La Tosca," and again in Milan for the Carnival of 1902, both at the Lirico, where he created the tenor rôle in Cilea's "Adriana Lecouvreur," and at La Scala, in Franchetti's "Germania." It was in this year that he also sang at Monte Carlo, with Melba—and was at once engaged for four seasons—and at Covent Garden, London, on May 14, as the Duke in "Rigoletto."

This London appearance was a great success so far as the public was concerned, though the critics in general did not recognize his possibilities. There had been but little advance publicity to herald his coming, and one London paper dismissed the performance the next morning with the bald statement that "the part of the Duke was carefully sung by M. Caruso." Throughout this season his singing won increasing applause at each of his appearances, but at that time his name on the boards never led to a rush on the box office.

During the winter of 1903-1904 he sang in Rome and in Lisbon, and it was on November 23, 1903, that he made his début at the Metropolitan Opera House in New York, in "Rigoletto."

His career in the United States—and it is with the United States and the Metropolitan Opera House in particular that he was most closely and intimately identified after his first appearance in this country in 1903—is a story in itself, and in order not to interrupt the sequence of his European successes, its consideration has been deferred till the following chapter.

Dating from his season in 1904, his popularity in London was immense, and he sang there every summer until the year 1907, when the management declined to reëngage him, pleading that his fee was excessive. This, however, did not interfere with his appearing in the British capital in concerts—notably the great Charity Concert in Albert Hall in 1908, during which year he also toured the English provinces—and at private entertainments, always eagerly sought and drawing immense audiences at all affairs of a public character.

It was his Rodolfo in Puccini's "La Bohème," which, more than any other single rôle, served to establish his popularity in London, though he also created the part of Pinkerton in Puccini's "Madame Butterfly" in that city, singing its music to perfection. In 1914 Caruso did accept a London engagement; it marked his last appearance in that city, and his singing in the last act of "Tosca" moved a critic to declare that: ". . . the mezza voce he used to present his legato passages thrilled the soul, as though the most glorious days of the past had come echoing back under a cupola of gold to remind us that never in our lifetime could we hope to hear anything comparable with that unique tenor which can only be summed up in one word—Caruso!"

Strange to say, among the great musical capitals of Europe, Paris is the one in which Caruso was least known, for he sang there no more than half a dozen times, usually at gala performances. In March, 1904, he took the part of Pinkerton in the creation of Puccini's "Madame Butterfly" at Monte Carlo;

but it was not until 1905, as a member of Sonzogno's Italian Company, that he appeared at
the Théâtre Sarah Bernhardt. Although he
was enthusiastically received by the Parisian
public, his other outstanding Paris appearances were few in number. In 1906, with
characteristic generosity, he interrupted a concert tour in order to sing at the Trocadero in
the city on the Seine for a benefit concert
which had been organized by the elder
Coquelin on behalf of the Association of Dramatic Artists. The French government expressed its appreciation of this action by making Caruso a chevalier of the Legion of
Honor. In 1912 he was heard at the Châtelet
Theatre in "Aïda," "Pagliacci," and Puccini's
"Manon Lescaut"; and in the same year he
created the rôle of Dick Johnson (Ramerrez)
in Puccini's "Fanciulla del West" at the
Paris Opéra.

In 1907 he included Leipsic, Hamburg, and
Berlin in a German *tournée* and was everywhere received with enthusiasm. In Berlin,
in particular, in 1907, 1910, and 1912, the
years of his appearances in that city, German
critical opinion was unanimously agreed that

no such powerful, high, and brilliant tenor voice had ever been heard before; and even those ancients who had heard the greatest artists of a generation or more could not recall a voice which could have measured itself beside Caruso's as regards perfected beauty, warmth, and genuine golden tone. The technique of his breath control—in which his system of rigorous vocal exercise played no unimportant part—together with his histrionic ability, was accorded the greatest praise. The same critical opinion attended his appearances in Munich, in Stuttgart, and in Hamburg as well.

In Vienna, the Vienna of the Hapsburgs, the way for Caruso's coming had been prepared by the sensational accounts of his fantastic American successes, and their—to European minds—incredible financial rewards, for some two years prior to his first appearance at the Hofoper. This took place in 1905, and though he won a victory in the rôle of the Duke of Mantua in "Rigoletto," at that time the rôle he sang best from a purely vocal point of view, it was, as one Viennese critic declared, "a victory without conquest."

Vienna did not really capitulate until he sang there in October, 1907. Then he was received with genuine enthusiasm, was obliged to repeat his canzonetta in "Rigoletto" three separate times, and even to repeat the solo at the beginning of the quartet, an unheard-of encore. But he won the Viennese completely and finally with his impersonation of Rodolfo in Puccini's "La Bohème"; for he was the original, living *bohémien* of Murger's novel, a fun-maker, full of practical jokes and wanton high spirits, a child, now laughing, now in tears. And in his singing he was not "merely" a poet.

The third rôle he presented to the Viennese audiences was that of Rhadames in "Aïda," carrying them away in the "Nile" act, in his B flat major aria, and in the duo, "Morir si pura e bella." The public fêted him as a singer, and paid him an homage it had accorded few singers before him. The tumult at the box-office, the storm on the galleries, the incredible activity of the ticket speculators, and the scenes at the "Operntürl," the exit of the Hofoper, where the famous singer's horses would undoubtedly have been taken from their traces had it not been an automobile that carried him away from the scene of his triumphs, were of nightly occurrence.

After 1907 Caruso appeared in Vienna every year, and endeared himself in particular with his Richard in "Un Ballo in Maschera," his Canio, and his Don José. When he appeared in "Carmen" for the first time in Vienna, the ordinarily well-bred Austrian public in its enthusiasm simply compelled him to a repetition in the middle of an act against his will. He had just ended his famous romance, and was kneeling at Carmen's feet, whose hand was caressingly laid upon his head. A tremendous burst of applause forced him to rise. There was a general cry of *bis, bis!* The singer indicated by a movement of his hand that a repetition was impossible for him, and again knelt. But the storm of applause kept on, and Caruso once more bowed his acknowledgments, refused the encore, and again prepared to continue the duet at Carmen's feet. The public, however, simply would not allow him to sing, though he made several further attempts. In the end the artist was obliged to resign himself, rise, and do as the public wished. And yet Caruso attained to even greater dramatic heights in the fourth act of the opera, when, with a cry like that of some ravening wild beast, he flung himself upon Carmen. It was at such moments that one realized that Caruso was not alone a model singer of bel canto, but a portrayer of human character, a creative artist of the most profound emotional passion and power. When Caruso sang in Vienna in 1913, before the War, he received $3,000 a performance, approximately 15,000 crowns, an immense sum for that city, and shortly before the War seats were practically sold at auction wherever he appeared in Austria or Germany.

It is worthy of remark that no matter where Caruso sang, whether in Russia or in Cuba, England or Mexico, France or Germany, Italy or the United States, the manner in which his singing united perfected tone and genuine emotion, a technique beyond compare, and a gift for dramatic impersonation which has rarely been equalled on the operatic stage, won for him all his auditors, irrespective of their nationality.

Chapter IV

THE CONQUEST OF THE NEW WORLD

THE American début of Enrico Caruso would undoubtedly have taken place earlier than it did, but for the fact that Maurice Grau resigned his post as impresario of the Metropolitan Opera House. After negotiating with Caruso for about a year, Grau had persuaded the tenor—then already famous in Europe but practically unknown in America—to sign a contract to join the Metropolitan forces. Heinrich Conried, who succeeded Grau at the Opera House and inherited this contract, was primarily a theatrical man and not a grand opera manager, and never having heard of the tenor, was at first not too eager to assume the responsibility of bringing over a singer unknown to him. There are many legends regarding Conried's final decision to invite Caruso to these shores, of which the most amusing one is to the effect that the impresario's Italian bootblack must share the honor, having made an appeal in the great tenor's favor. As a matter of fact, it was Maurice Grau's sound judgment, together with information freshly gathered, that overcame Conried's reluctance; and Enrico Caruso made his American début at the Metropolitan Opera House on November 23, 1903, as the Duke in "Rigoletto," Madame Sembrich singing the rôle of Gilda.

The great audience that filled the Metropolitan that memorable night of Caruso's career had not come to welcome the new tenor: the management had done nothing to arouse curiosity about him. Madame Sembrich, who had already become a great favorite with New York opera audiences, was warmly welcomed; so was the new conductor, Signor Vigna. But when Enrico Caruso entered upon the stage, all he received from the audience was a respectful silence. This cold reception would have dismayed many a singer, especially if he was accustomed to being lionized in the capitals of Europe. Caruso, however, did not permit the audience's indifference to ruffle him. He was determined to win recognition. He sang with great care, intent on having his instrument under complete control. Before that performance of "Rigoletto" was concluded, Caruso had conquered the audience.

The following day the critics hailed Caruso as a great artist with a wonderful vocal organ. The indifference of the audience, when he had first made his entrance, now added glory and dramatic interest to his triumph.

"Strange to say," wrote the *Post,* "whereas the new conductor, Mr. Vigna, was greeted with a round of applause when he took his seat in the lowered orchestral space, where he disappeared from sight, not a hand was raised for Mr. Caruso when he became visible on the stage. Nobody seemed to know him; nor is that strange, for he is a young man—only thirty years of age—and he was hardly known, even in Italy, until five years ago. Having established his fame at Milan and Genoa, he sang for two seasons in St. Petersburg, and then went to South America, where his popularity soon induced the manager to double the price of his seats. In London he subsequently made a sensational success, which led to his engagement for New York. Real tenors, Italian or otherwise, are extremely scarce, and

Mr. Caruso is in demand in every city which has opera; we simply got him because in New York we have 'the high-salary crime'—a crime which has its advantages.

"If Mr. Caruso was received in silence, the loud applause which greeted his first air, *Questa o quella,* made ample amends. And the enthusiasm grew from act to act, culminating in an ovation after *La donna è mobile.* True, he exaggerated its catchpenny effect by his vocal flourishes at the end; but the changes of pace he introduced in the melody made it seem less offensive than usual, and his phrasing, here as in the other numbers, was remarkably artistic and refined. Like some of his famous colleagues, he was not at his best early in the evening; but as he warmed up to his task his voice was revealed as a genuine tenor of excellent quality, which it will be a pleasure to hear again. To hear him sing duos with Mme. Sembrich was a rare treat."

Not yet had Caruso reached those heights of perfection in the mastery of his voice and in the subtlety of his interpretations which were later to make him supreme in the realm of song. But the vital quality of sincerity,

which makes the artist's work effective and
convincing, was there; it was the predominant
characteristic of Caruso's singing and it was
that which roused so keen an interest in his
future. That it was his large vocal power
and the ringing tones of his upper range which
stirred the greatest number of his hearers,
there is no doubting; but the keener and more
cultivated listeners were impressed by the delicate and finely spun phrasing, by the exquisite
musical delivery, and by that manliness which
reveals the sincerity of an artist.

The musical writer for the *Times* recognized
in Caruso a sterling singer whose art was not
only charged with passion but also controlled
by intelligence. He wrote about the début:

"It signalized the first appearance of one
of the most important of Mr. Conried's new
artists, one upon whom much will depend during the coming season—Enrico Caruso, who
took the part of the Duke. He made a highly
favorable impression, and he went far to sub-
stantiate the reputation that had preceded
him in this country. He is an Italian in all
his fiber, and his acting and singing are characteristic of what Italy now affords in those

arts. His voice is purely a tenor in its quality, of high range, and of large power, but inclined to take on the 'white' quality in its upper ranges when he lets it forth. In mezza voce it has expressiveness and flexibility, and when so used its beauty is most apparent. Mr. Caruso appeared last evening capable of intelligence and of passion in both his singing and his acting, and gave reason to believe in his value as an acquisition to the company."

The musical critic of the *Sun* was impressed by Caruso's finer qualities as a vocal artist. He said in part:

"Mr. Caruso, the new tenor, made a thoroughly favorable impression, and will probably grow into the firm favor of this public. He has a pure tenor voice of fine quality and sufficient range and power. It is a smooth and mellow voice and is without the typical Italian bleat. Mr. Caruso has a natural and free delivery and his voice carries well without forcing. He phrased his music tastefully and showed considerable refinement of style.

"His clear and pealing high tones set the bravos wild with delight, but connoisseurs of singing saw more promise for the season in his mezza voce and his manliness."

Caruso had scored a success, but one that fell far short of the great enthusiasm he was afterward to arouse. Profound as was the impression he had made, little did the people who heard him sing that night realize that the new tenor was soon to become one of the pillars of the Metropolitan Opera House, nay, its mainstay for nearly a generation. For Caruso introduced at the Metropolitan a new standard of vocal art, a singing so rich and vibrant in its delivery that it seemed to overshadow the art of all those master-singers who had preceded him in that famous house of music. There were memories of great voices at the Metropolitan when Enrico. Caruso arrived; there may have been voices of greater power; there may have been voices of greater agility; but none had possessed the infinite gradations of tone color, nor the poignant utterance of Caruso's glorious organ. Even at that time he carried his voice with great skill throughout a wide compass and sang each tone, from the lowest to the highest, with a purity and roundness that captivated his auditors. The voice he had brought to the Metropolitan was a tenor of fine texture, both velvety and opulent in quality; but it was the warmth and magnetism of his tones that moved his hearers and compelled their enthusiasm. At all events, after his début Caruso's art was closely watched not only by all the New York critics but by the general public as well.

The many admirers the new tenor had won at his first performance were very eager to hear his Rodolfo in Puccini's "La Bohème," which he was scheduled to sing a few days later. But the sharp weather which sometimes visits New York in late November brought them disappointment. Caruso had contracted a severe cold and could not appear. His sudden indisposition caused the management of the Metropolitan a good deal of uneasiness; they felt that here was a popular tenor upon whom they could not rely. The new impresario, Heinrich Conried, soon learned, however, that Enrico Caruso was an artist who disliked to disappoint his audiences. In fact, although not in fit vocal condition to sing Rhadames, Caruso consented to appear in "Aïda" just a week after his début, and the plaudits that were showered on him were more enthusiastic and tumultuous than they had been at his first appearance.

"The greatest interest," said the *Times,* "was felt in Mr. Caruso's assumption of the part of Rhadames, and though he evidently had not recovered from the troubles that put so sudden a check upon his career here after his first appearance, he materially deepened the favorable impression he then made. He was clearly singing with circumspection and care, especially in the first act of the opera, and seldom ventured to put forth the full power of his voice. But in the very manner in which he did this he proved the remarkable mastery he possesses over his organ, and the skill of his vocal technique, the manifold resources he possesses to make every effect count, even against the most unfavorable influences. He sang with some evidences of effort when he did sing with his full power. With all his reserve, however, the quality, the flexibility, and the expressive capacity of his voice beautified everything he did. His action was forceful and authoritative, so far as force and authority come into the purview of

Rhadames' experience. There were passion and conviction in his interpretation of the hated lover, and everywhere the marks of the adept in stagecraft. It was an admirable performance and commanded not only the enthusiastic plaudits of the cooler portions of the audience, but also the frenzied 'bravos' of his compatriots, who were present in large numbers. After the third act there were scenes of tumultuous enthusiasm."

The musical writer for the *Post* was impressed by Caruso's style and refined phrasing. He wrote: "And last, not least, was the Rhadames of Signor Caruso, whose singing of *Celeste Aïda* was followed by a great outburst of applause; and he deserved it. Reports from abroad did not exaggerate the merits of this tenor. He is what has so long been looked for—a successor to Campanini, and more, too. While his voice is not so reliable as Campanini's, it is infused with more ardor and has more dramatic power, while being equally beautiful in quality when at its best."

The critic of the *Sun* was no less impressed by the qualities of Caruso's singing. In his review of the performance of "Aïda" he said:

"Mr. Caruso, the new Italian tenor, confirmed the good impression he made at his début. He saved himself a good deal in the early part of the opera, which was wise in view of his recent indisposition, but this gave him an opportunity to show the resources of his art in *Celeste Aïda.* He sang the air quietly but tastefully and with good effect. In the Nile scene he let himself out and made the bravos wild with delight."

In the *Tribune,* Caruso's song art was also praised. The critic wrote: "The latter (Signor Caruso) was plainly still suffering from the indisposition which worked such shipwreck in the representation of 'La Bohème' last Friday night, and 'Rigoletto' on Saturday afternoon. But his skill in overcoming the drawback helped to a keener appreciation of his knowledge of the art of singing, and invited still greater admiration for the superb beauty of his voice. The pleasure which his singing gives is exquisite, scarcely leaving room for curious shortcomings touching his limitations."

A few days later Caruso sang the rôle of Cavaradossi in "Tosca." He displayed the same skill as a vocal artist and as an interpreter of character which he had disclosed in his first two appearances at the Opera House. He sang the music of the young revolutionist with warmth and color, and the famous aria *E lucevan le stelle* brought forth rounds and rounds of applause. But Caruso had not yet revealed to American opera-goers all of the vocal artistry and eloquence that he had at his command. Thus far he had been heard in but one rôle to which he had done full justice—the Duke in "Rigoletto," which he had sung with a charm, grace, and nonchalance that captivated his hearers.

In "Aïda" and "Tosca" he had not been quite himself, because he dared not give full sway to his golden voice. But by the time he made his fourth appearance, he had completely regained his vocal powers and he infused into his song such art and beauty that he was unstintedly accorded the supreme place among singing men.

"Mr. Caruso," wrote the *Times,* "showed yesterday afternoon for the first time since he has been in this country the supreme beauty of his voice and the perfection of his style when he is at his best. He took the part of

Rodolfo—the part which he was prevented from assuming in the first week of the season by the throat trouble that temporarily put him out of commission in Mr. Conried's forces and that left its traces after he had returned to service.

"Mr. Caruso plays the part of Puccini's Latin Quarter hero with especial sympathy and presents a figure of unusual attractiveness. . . . It has distinction in its kind bonhomie, humor, pathos. But it was most striking in its musical side. Mr. Caruso's voice has never sounded so deliciously pure, rich, and smooth, so clear and warm in its upper tones, so full and free in its emission without a trace of the 'white' and open quality that was objected to at his first appearance.

"He sang with great fervor and passion, and poured out his voice with prodigality. Now we know what Mr. Caruso's voice really is. As it was displayed yesterday afternoon, it was such a one as has not been enjoyed here for a long time, and enjoyment of it was raised to a higher power by the skill with which it was put at the service of a keenly felt dramatic conception."

In that same season (1903-1904) Caruso appeared in four other operas: "I Pagliacci," "La Traviata," "Lucia di Lammermoor," and "L'Elisir d'Amore." As Canio in "Pagliacci," he evinced his versatile genius; his impersonation of the tragic Pagliaccio—a species of strolling clown who is often a comedian, a singer, and a pantomimist—made known that he was not only a great singer, but an actor of fine intelligence too. It was a performance instinct with musicianship as well as with unusual histrionic ability. To this work of Leoncavallo's, the only genuine masterpiece the composer was destined to give to the world, Caruso brought a personality of such power and magnetism that he and the opera were from that time on inseparable. Caruso, by his great acting and singing, made the rôle of Canio his own. "I Pagliacci" had been sung at the Metropolitan Opera House before Caruso became a member of that company, but no one before Caruso had given full expression to the vocal and dramatic possibilities in Canio. True, Caruso himself had not yet reached the eminence as a singer and creator of character that he was to achieve after more years of diligent work, the high tide of art which finally made his interpretation of Canio a marvel of the operatic stage. But the fire and passion, the sardonic humor and bitter irony, and the tragic note which he breathed into the rôle even at his first appearance in it at the Metropolitan did much to enhance the dramatic significance of the opera. It was after Caruso had infused into the pulsating rhythm and melody of "Pagliacci" the eloquence of his glorious voice and the vitality of his dramatic style that Leoncavallo's great work attained in America the popularity it deserves.

As Alfredo in "La Traviata," Caruso scored another success. He sang his airs in a masterly manner and seemed to put the charm of novelty into whatever music he chose to interpret. No aria that he sang sounded antiquated or colorless, so marvelous were the effects of his magic art. Even the puppet heroes of the old operas Caruso could transform into real beings with emotions and passions; and as a result of this revivification their utterance in song acquired a new interest. It is thus that Caruso made Edgardo in "Lucia di Lammermoor" seem real and human. Likewise, as Nemorino in "L'Elisir d' Amore," Caruso put so much feeling and pathos into the music of the futile and ungraceful lover that it became of vital significance to the audience. He enraptured his hearers with his heart-felt and delicately-nuanced rendering of the famous airs *Una furtiva lagrima* and *Quanto e bella.* Flowery and old-fashioned melodies took on a new glamour when Caruso ennobled them by his fluent delivery and refined style, and he sang these two with a genuine lyrical beauty which never degenerated into whining sentimentality. Even in their most feeble moments, his singing imparted to them virility and body. And as for the rhetorical passion with which most of the old arias are replete, the stirring appeal of Caruso's ringing tones made even that affected ardor convincing.

The element in the song art which made his rendering of the old arias so remarkable was an unusual technical equipment. His voice was not only extraordinarily flexible, so that the tone gradations between a pianissimo and a fortissimo were infinite in variety, but it was just as preëminent in its agility. This perfection of vocal technique made it possible for Caruso to sing the florid passages of the arias with a brilliance which evoked the versatile artists of the golden age of song. No such fioritura singing had been heard from a tenor voice. Indeed, Caruso executed the flourishing runs and cadenzas so brilliantly and with such clean-cut agility that his audience remained breathless at his vocal artistry. These were the qualities in Caruso's singing—the warmth and magnetism of his tones, the compelling expressiveness of his style, the great suppleness of his delivery, and his unusual dramatic powers—that foretold, after his first season at the Metropolitan Opera House, a great American career.

It is curious, however, that in the course of the South American engagement at Buenos Aires which Caruso filled during the same year, he was given quite a cool reception. The opera subscribers there were disappointed when he appeared in Boito's "Mefistofele," and even requested the management not to renew its contract with him for the following year. But by the time the following year had arrived, Caruso had so firmly established himself in the favor of his American audiences with "La Gioconda," "Lucrezia Borgia," "Les Huguenots," "Un Ballo in Maschero," as well as with the operas in which he had appeared the first season, and was now in such demand, both in America and Europe, that Buenos Aires did not have an opportunity to hear him again for twelve years. It was not until 1915, when the new Colon Opera House in that city had been completed, that the management succeeded in reengaging Caruso; and it now had to pay him 350,000 francs for ten performances, instead of the 30,000 francs he had previously received for an entire season.

During Caruso's second season at the Metropolitan his popularity with the public grew tremendously. On the night when he sang all the seats were sold, and there was always a long line of standees waiting to secure tickets for the performance. Before the second season was over Caruso was no longer merely a favorite opera singer: he had become a popular idol. No singer at the Metropolitan had ever fired the public imagination as Caruso had done. For the great majority of people, he and the Metropolitan Opera House had become one. Even the Wagner enthusiasts, who would have been overjoyed to have so glorious a voice to reveal the music of Sigfried, Sigmund, and Tristan to the world, reluctantly admitted that Caruso made irresistible whatever music he sang.

On March 5, 1906, Caruso appeared for the first time at the Metropolitan as Don José in "Carmen." "The theatre was crowded," wrote the musical critic of the *Sun,* " . . . Signor Caruso was singing Don José for the first time here and making his second appearance in French. In these days, when New York is no longer opera mad, but Caruso mad, this was sufficient occasion for the audience and its enthusiasm. It may be said at the outset, for the comfort of the tenor's admirers, that he put another success to his credit."

Such is the popularity that Caruso had won toward the end of his third season in New York. Prior to his appearance in "Carmen," he had sung in four other operas for the first time at the Metropolitan; he had opened the season with "La Favorita"; the following week he had added "La Sonnambula"; and

later in the season "Faust" and "Marta." His
beautiful cantilena singing found a most suitable outlet in Donizetti's melodious "La
Favorita," and the musical significance of
"La Sonnambula" and of "Marta" awoke
under his masterly vocal art. In "Faust"
Caruso's singing was notable, but he was singing in French for the first time, so that he did
not attain his usual high level in Gounod's
opera. Moreover, Caruso had already set up
so high a standard that his audiences would
have nothing short of perfection. "Faust"
left some dissatisfaction among the more ardent of his admirers.

So the announcement that Caruso would
sing Don José occasioned much discussion as
to the tenor's qualifications to sing French
opera. The opera-goers who lacked confidence in Caruso's powers were destined to be
disappointed. His Don José was a triumph.
Vocally and dramatically, the tenor gave an
exceedingly finished performance that deeply
stirred the audience. In Caruso's interpretation, Don José became the truly tragic lover
that he is, not merely a stage puppet; there
was remarkable acting in his portrayal of the

unhappy soldier dominated by a passion which
leads him to destruction. But Caruso's interpretation of Bizet's exquisite music and pro-
pulsive rhythms was even more striking than
his acting. He thrilled the audience with his
singing of the famous romance in the second
act, *La fleur que tu m'avais jetée,* leading up
to a climax of overwhelming dramatic and
vocal power at the end of the air with *Carmen,
je t'aime.* The artistic phrasing, the dynamic
contrasts and gradations, the beauty of tone,
and the warmth of passion with which Caruso
sang this exquisite tale of the flower was alone
sufficient to rank him as the foremost of all
Don Josés.

His superb acting and singing in "Carmen"
made ample amends for his less perfect performance earlier in the season in "Faust."
There were no longer any doubts as to whether
he might be merely a master in Italian operas;
in fact, his great success in "Carmen" fore-
shadowed his later triumph in "Samson et
Dalila" and in what was, alas, to be his last
creation, "La Juive." Caruso's was, indeed,
a versatile genius; and had he been called upon
at the Metropolitan to enlarge still further

the scope of his repertory he would have achieved unique success in many other rôles. At one time there were rumors that he might appear in "Lohengrin": now we can only speculate about what wondrous music would have been poured out had Enrico Caruso chosen to sing Lohengrin or Tristan.

It is difficult to divide Caruso's career into periods when he sang either lyric, semi-dramatic, or dramatic rôles. It was only at the very beginning of his career that he confined himself to parts written primarily for the lyric tenor; for after he had gained a foothold in the world of opera, he essayed to sing rôles which required dramatic vocal power. Although Caruso never sought power for its own sake, he steadily cultivated the intensity of his voice with a view to attaining the necessary vocal power to be able to sing dramatic rôles with ease. For he knew full well the danger of straining the vocal organs. That was why he did not attempt, for example, Samson or Eléazer until he felt that the power of his voice had been sufficiently developed to do justice to these two mighty rôles. Caruso had always wished to sing Verdi's "Otello"; but, season after season, he postponed appearing in it, so that he might still develop the vocal resources essential for that great part. How many tenors in the annals of opera have been so conscientious about their art? For it was, with Caruso, a straight question of art; he was well aware of the fact that there can be no beautiful singing when the vocal organs are strained or forced.

Generally speaking, the first period of his career at the Metropolitan may be called his lyric one. His rôles were, more or less, the essentially lyric parts in the repertory operas which had made him famous in Italy and in the other principal countries of Europe. But Caruso aspired to more than the honors of a purely lyric tenor. He was too devoted to the art he loved to wish to forego the great dramatic rôles of the operatic repertory, rôles he was not only vocally, but also histrionically, so uniquely qualified to present. Thus, in what might be called his second period, he began to add the more dramatic characterizations to what in the end was to be a magnificent repertory of more than seventy rôles— some of which he never sang, though he had acquired and perfected them, since he was never averse to studying a new part.

The perfected control of so large a repertory, including some of the most difficult rôles in all opera, testifies to the wide range of his conception. His ambition, successfully realized, to shine in the more dramatic and heroic rôles of opera led, through diligent practice, to the development of that powerful tone of his middle range which in "Armide," "Les Huguenots," "Le Prophète," "La Juive," and "I Pagliacci"—though his Canio in the last-named opera was a part which he sang during all three of his periods —aided him in securing such brilliant effects of declamation. It was in connection with this middle range of his voice that he once said: "In a legato phrase the 'cello in particular, when well played, is almost identical with the human voice. It often inspires the tones of my middle range, and I often lead up those tones just as the 'cellist does on his A string."

The quality of Caruso's voice broadened considerably and became more intense with the passing years; but it never lost the golden timbre which distinguished it from every other tenor voice. Though, as he tended more and more to the dramatic, he sang such rôles as the Duke of Mantua and Rodolfo less often; though a new method of attack, more vigorous and spontaneous (at times well-nigh explosive) marked the transition to his last period—inaugurated, let us say, by his wonderful Samson in Saint-Saëns' "Samson et Dalila"; nevertheless the ringing brilliancy, the rounded glory, of the tones of his upper range did not desert him.

This last period of Caruso's artistic activity reveals him at his greatest. Here the matured, perfected artist made deliberate choice of those rôles of heroic scope and possibility which not even his glorious voice could infuse with dramatic conviction without the brain and the actor that had studied its perfect blending with the stage presentation of the character portrayed. Was there ever a more striking picture to be found on the operatic stage than his Samson, despoiled of his strength, the mock of the Philistines, blind and chained to the treadmill? In his John of Leyden, in "Le Prophète," the madness of the anabaptist

King of Sion, his depraved and bloodthirsty
character, was actually forgotten when Caruso, in the fourth act, portrayed his demoniac
renunciation of his mother in a manner at
once so grandiose and so majestic that one was
almost inclined to believe in the pretender and
his mission. And in "La Juive" the over-
whelmingly dramatic conception of revenge
personified by Caruso as Eléazar in the latter's aria in the second act, and the emotional
tenseness of the great aria of the fourth act,
in which he asks God's guidance, was something no other tenor of his day could equal.
It is characteristic of Caruso's attention to
detail that while he was studying the rôle of
Eléazar he coached with one of the foremost
Yiddish actors of New York in order to make
himself letter-perfect in every inflection of
Jewish orthodox manner and custom de-
manded by the part.

Certain operas which Caruso created at the
Metropolitan Opera House will always be associated with his name, and that less because
of the works themselves than for what he made
of them by his singing of his own rôles. There
was his Nadir, for example, in Bizet's "Les
Pêcheurs de Perles." Though there is but

little incident in this operatic tale of the loves of two Cingalese pearl-fishers for the priestess Leila, and though its music—in spite of its charm and originality—is not so very characteristic of Bizet's genius, Caruso, by the manner in which he handled the few scenes of real dramatic force, gave the score an unexpected unity and significance. And all who think that Caruso's stage victories were won without effort would change their views if they knew how he worked to create the title rôle of Charpentier's "Julien" (February 26, 1914). It is a question whether, taken purely as a rôle, Caruso ever gave a finer and a more sincere interpretation, one based on harder study or greater mental and vocal toil. That "Julien" could not maintain its place in the repertory was not the fault of the tenor.

After Caruso had appeared in "Carmen" in 1906, he sang seven other new rôles at the Metropolitan during the two remaining seasons of Conried's régime.[1] The first opera

[1] 1906-07
 Dec. 5.—"Fedora"
 Jan. 11.—"L'Africaine"
 Jan. 18.—"Manon Lescaut"
 Feb. 11.—"Madame Butterfly"
1907-08
 Nov. 18.—"Adriana Lecouvreur"
 Dec. 6.—"Iris"
 Feb. 26.—"Il Trovatore"

which was revived for him during Signor
Gatti-Casazza's administration of the Metropolitan was Massenet's "Manon," February 3,
1909; and the last one was "La Juive," on
November 22, 1919. During this period of
ten years Caruso lent the prestige of his art
to thirteen rôles, including "La Juive" and
"Manon." [1] Had the management not called
upon Caruso for frequent repetitions of many
of the favorite operas, no doubt he would have
added more new rôles to his repertory at the

[1] 1908-09
    Feb. 3.—"Manon"
    Apr. 3.—"Cavalleria Rusticana"
   1909-10
    Jan. 22.—"Germania"
   1910-11
    Nov. 14.—"Armide"
    Dec. 10.—"Fanciulla del West"
   1911-12
    . . . .
   1912-13
    . . . .
   1913-14
    Feb. 26.—"Julien"
   1914-15
    . . . .
   1915-16
    Nov. 15.—"Samson et Dalila"
   1916-17
    Nov. 13.—"Les Pêcheurs de Perles"
   1917-18
    Jan. 12.—"Lodoletta"
    Feb. 7.—"Le Prophète"
    Mar. 14.—"L'Amore dei Tre Re"
   1918-19
    Nov. 15.—"La Forza del Destino"
   1919-20
    Nov. 22.—"La Juive"

Metropolitan. At all events, enthusiastically as he was received in whatever opera he made his appearance, Caruso nevertheless continually sought to enlarge the number of rôles in his already extensive repertory. Which accounts for his singing of Renaud in "Armide," a part that was not quite suitable for him, although the *Post* praised him for his endeavor.

"As for Mr. Caruso," it said, "he deserves great credit for being willing to assume a rôle lying so far outside his usual sphere. His Renaud is the fourth he has sung here in French, the first in an opera written by a German. It cannot be said that in appearance he realized one's idea of an invincible Crusader; nor did he sing his first numbers with his usual luscious tones and fervent style. It was not till the last act was reached that the audience heard the real Caruso; and the real Caruso is—well, everybody knows what he is —he is Caruso. That's all."

As Des Grieux in Massenet's "Manon," however, Caruso was himself from the beginning to the very end of the opera. He recreated Des Grieux, and he infused into this part, both in his singing and acting, a warmth and sincerity rarely found on the operatic stage. All opera-goers who heard him sing *Fuyez, douce image* or *Un rêve* heard these two gems of Massenet's re-created.

In his last two creations at the Metropolitan, in "La Forza del Destino" and in "La Juive," both operas especially revived for Caruso, the vocal artistry and the dramatic utterance impressively revealed a great singer still at the zenith of his powers. As Don Alvaro in "La Forza del Destino," which Caruso sang here for the first time on November 15, 1918, his vocal art moved so profoundly the late James Gibbons Huneker that he wrote in the *Times* the following morning: "There is one word with which to characterize Caruso's singing—glorious. That pianissimo whisper when lying on the couch in Act III showed us the master of artistic vocalism. A lovely legato, and of a sweet sonorousness. He interpreted the rôle as it should be interpreted, robustly. He was the impetuous soldier, the ardent lover. A stirring impersonation."

As Eléazar in "La Juive," Caruso achieved a great dramatic interpretation—perhaps the greatest of his operatic career. We have already mentioned the painstaking care with which he studied this rôle, so that he could portray the character faithfully and sincerely. And he succeeded. His make-up was a marvel of imaginative conception. He did more than merely depict an old orthodox Jew; he discovered Eléazar's very soul. There was characterization in every gesture and in every inflection of the voice. Small wonder that his impersonation was hailed as a wonderful dramatic and musical achievement. On the day following the first performance (November 22, 1919), the musical critic of the *Sun* paid Caruso this richly deserved tribute:

"Enrico Caruso, who began life as a lyric tenor, aerial of tone and prone to the youthful passions of operatic heroes, is now a full fledged tenore robusto, battling with the agonies of fatherhood, the subtleties of political plot, and the plangent utterances of French recitative. . . . No one who is familiar with the achievement of the most popular singer of this time would expect to be told that he met all the requirements of such a rôle as Eléazar. Nor would any one of the mil-

lion devoted admirers of his voice care. . . .
Therefore he commands the respect and admiration of all who regard operatic creations
as of more import in art than their inter-
preters, for he has again and again shown himself a sincere seeker after genuine dramatic
results. His Julien, his Renaud in 'Armide,'
and his John of Leyden in 'The Prophet'
brought him honor, and his Eléazar in 'La
Juive' will be remembered as one of his highest flights.

"He conceived the part in earnest study and
he sang and acted with an art as far removed
as possible from that of his more familiar Italian rôles. There was dignity in his declamation and beauty in his cantilena. His chanting in
the second act was a lyric utterance of exquisite character, while his delivery of the pealing
air of the fourth act might have excited the
envy of Nourrit himself.

"The revival of 'La Juive' was worth while,
if only to add this impersonation to Mr. Caruso's successes; and if the opera retains a
hold on the public interest it will owe most of
its fortune to the artistic effort of the famous
tenor."

On March 22, 1919, Enrico Caruso sang at a special gala performance at the Metropolitan Opera House, celebrating the twenty-fifth year of his career, the proceeds of the performance going to the Metropolitan Opera Company Emergency Fund. At this silver jubilee celebration the Mayor and other prominent New Yorkers paid tribute to Caruso's artistic achievements. By way of tokens of gratitude, Caruso received a testimonial of recognition on an illuminated parchment from thirty-five families holding boxes in the "Golden Horseshoe," a great gold medal from the management, an American flag from the City of New York, and numerous gifts from his colleagues.

During eighteen years in all, one might say up to the very day of his death—for he had arranged with Signor Gatti-Casazza to return for the season of 1921-1922 only a few days before he sailed for Italy in May, 1921—Enrico Caruso was the *tenore assoluto* of the Metropolitan Opera House. Though on several occasions legitimate alarm had been felt about the condition of his throat, his supremacy was uncontested to the last, and he died as he had lived, the unchallenged holder of the leadership he had so deservedly won.

The full and free mastery of so many different rôles naturally prompted the question, often asked Caruso, as to which he liked best. He always denied a preference: "I have no favorite rôles," he said, "and I think no real artist should have them.   The singer who selects rôles of a certain type and kind, and wants to sing no others, is not a great artist. He is a specialist."

As has been the case with some of the greatest artists, Caruso, though he may not have suffered from "stage fright" in the ordinary sense of the word, was usually intensely nervous, "keyed up," before his performance.   He often spoke of being "scared to death," and of feeling unable to sing until he had reached his dressing room and donned his costume. (Before appearing on the stage he would vocalize for about five minutes.)   On one occasion he even exclaimed: "Whenever I sing I feel as if some one were waiting to seize my position, to destroy Caruso!   And I must fight to hold my own."

Speaking of a performance of "La Juive"

in Brooklyn, he declared: "The moment I
appeared on the stage and beheld the audience, among them Bonci, I realized that I *had*
to sing—and then a miracle happened. Some
unseen power seemed to unlock the compart-
ment within me which holds my voice and I
sang. I sang with all the power within me.
You see, we artists must struggle desperately
to get to the top, and once there, we must hold
on with all the strength we have. For once
we slip, the journey down is fast. Yet, once
in the proper atmosphere, my voice appears,
and then it is up to me to make the most
of it."

With the exception of a few more or less
private engagements, Caruso, contrary to the
usual custom of opera singers, for a long time
refused to appear on the concert stage. It
was not until May, 1917, that he consented to
"try" a few concerts. The Cincinnati Sym-
phony Orchestra was engaged, and concerts
in Cincinnati, Toledo, and Pittsburgh were
triumphantly successful. Thereafter he made
concert tours in 1918, 1919, and 1920, visiting a number of American cities; and in the
fall of 1920 his most extensive tour took him

as far west as Denver. This tour opened in the Montreal Arena, on September 28, where he sang to an audience of over seven thousand people, and established what is considered the world's record for concert receipts in a single night, a total of $28,700.

Despite his great and abiding popularity, and the fact that whenever he came before an audience he gave it his best, Caruso had few illusions. He knew that the great public is fickle, and that the most sincere and beautiful work of an artist, especially if that artist, like himself, be placed on a lonely pinnacle of fame, does not always receive due acknowledgment. He never tired of work, however, and he always attributed his great achievements to his untiring industry.

Only a few months before his death Caruso epitomized his own rules of success: "Success is due to real work along one's natural calling. Work, work, and still more work, makes the fine singer. Laziness in preparatory work makes the failure."

Chapter V

CARUSO THE MAN

THE "off-stage" personality of Caruso, his richly human character with its inherent manly qualities, was such as to endear him to all who came in contact with him. For his musical and artistic temper went hand in hand with an accessibility to every generous emotion—a natural, normal capacity for enjoyment in his family life and in the company of his numerous friends.

Two sons, Rodolfo and Enrico—of whom the first served as a soldier in the Italian army during the Great War—had been born to Caruso of his union with Ada Ciachetti, a singer associated with him in opera at Treviso and Bologna. This union was, however, not a happy one. In August, 1918, Caruso married Miss Dorothy Park Benjamin, the daughter of a well-known New York lawyer, and in this marriage—his little daughter Gloria, whom he idolized, was born about a year later

—he found the happiness previously denied him.

During his eighteen years in this country Caruso had become not only thoroughly Americanized, but a representative and very popular figure in American life, especially in the life of New York City. America had whole-heartedly accepted him as her own. Whenever he appeared in public every eye was fixed on him. Crowds beset him on the streets, in railway stations, in the lobbies of theaters, in fact whenever he appeared outside his rooms in the Hotel Knickerbocker, where he lived until that hostelry—much to his regret—was converted into an office building and he took up his residence in the Hotel Vander-bilt. His summers, save when engagements or the War precluded, he usually spent in his beautiful Villa Bellosguardo, at Lastra-Signa, a village near Florence. But the greater part of his time was spent in New York, and it was New York that was most intimately associated with his public and domestic life from the night of his successful début, in 1903, at the Metropolitan Opera House.

By 1919 he had become so thorough a New

Yorker that he accepted with pleasure an honorary appointment as Captain in the New York Police Reserve, bought himself a fine tailor-made uniform, and proudly displayed the gold badge of authority on his chest. He declared that none of the medals bestowed on him in the past gave him the thrill his police badge did, and that he felt irresistibly inclined to go straight over to the Metropolitan Opera House and arrest some one, any one, by way of showing his authority.

Notable is the fact that he was as popular with his colleagues, the other artists at the Opera House, as he was with the world at large. He was, in fact, more than popular with them—he was genuinely beloved; and affection in an institution where artistic bickerings and jealousies, though usually withheld from the public, are none the less frequent, is a convincing testimonial to one's qualities as a human being. Caruso's position, to be sure, was a unique one; yet it is not always the artist who stands on the highest rung of the ladder of fame who is most willing to aid his lesser colleague.

From solo singers to the "supers" who

helped carry him in the palanquin in which he entered in "Aïda," and who took care never to "dump" him upon the stage, all knew him as a self-sacrificing, amiable friend, and his greatest joy was to help young beginners out of their difficulties. In one performance of "Rigoletto," when a small, delicate Gilda was appearing for the first time and in her excitement could develop no more than a trembling soft tone, Caruso, as her partner in the duet, toned down his own voice to suit the girl's lesser tonal fulness and thus restored her confidence, refusing to take advantage of her momentary lack of a bigger volume of tone. Incidents of this kind were numerous in his career.

The humorous outbreaks in which he was accustomed to indulge when he received a curtain call at the close of an act, and which have been censured by those who were ignorant of what really called them forth, were in reality no more than the expression of his overpowering relief at having once more triumphed over the initial doubts and artistic nervousness which preceded his every public appearance.

It was his custom after the Christmas performance at the Metropolitan to play Santa Claus, passing out gold pieces from a large pouch to all members of the company and to every one connected with the stage. Though in physical agony at the last performance he ever gave—"La Juive" on Christmas Eve of 1920—and though in his efforts to sing on the stage he had burst the plaster bands with which his chest had been tightly wrapped, he did not forget his old custom, but at the first opportunity, sick as he was, began passing out his gold pieces as usual.

His generosity was unparalleled, as is proved by the estate he left, small in proportion to his immense earnings. No deserving appeal left him cold. He gave, and gave and gave unweariedly, wherever he felt that he was alleviating misery, aiding an artist in his struggle to climb the heights, or even merely bringing a little happiness into lives ordinarily drab and colorless. He was the first to put his name, and always for a sizable sum, to any contribution list which reached him at the Opera or elsewhere. He was always ready to sing at a benefit concert for any worthy cause, and was liberal in his services for patriotic objects during the War.

One night a wigmaker was at work in his dressing-room at the Opera, and saw Caruso take a roll of bills from his pocket and throw it on the table while he changed his costume.

"I wish I had one of those," said the man wistfully.

"What would you do with it if you had?" asked the tenor.

"Well," said the wigmaker, "I'd take my wife on a trip to see her mother."

"Here's one," said Caruso, as he peeled a $500 bill from the roll and handed it to the man.

His heart was as big as his voice. No more sincere tribute to his personal qualities could be adduced than that paid him by Edward Siedle, technical director of the Metropolitan Opera House Company. "Speaking for the people behind the scenes, the electricians, the scene shifters, the stage hands, property men, costumers and doormen, he was the embodiment of kindness, good humor and friendliness. . . . Even the least of the workmen felt his kindness. As he passed each one there was always a salutation—no commonness, no loss of personal dignity—just friendly good fellowship. . . . I could tell you incidents without number of cases where Caruso stepped into the breach and helped needy persons. . . . In all the years he was here I can remember no unpleasant incident for which he was responsible."

If his generous charity might be called the first of his hobbies, his others were by no means unworthy of the great artist. For caricature, the drawing of cartoons, he had a veritable passion. He drew at his luncheon table at the Hotel Knickerbocker, limning the faces of others in the room; he sketched behind the scenes at the Metropolitan, or among his friends, or when he was being interviewed; he had pencil and paper at hand on all occasions. He prided himself as much on his skill as a caricaturist as he did on his singing. And the collection of his caricatures, published in 1914, shows that he was justified in that pride.

It has been said, indeed, that had Caruso given up his operatic career and devoted his life to drawing caricatures, he would have become just as great a world figure in the other art. To the close student of Caruso's work as a caricaturist this statement will appear far from extravagant. For there are few artists practicing caricature who can equal Caruso, and still fewer who are his superiors. The remarkable quality in Caruso's draftsmanship was his capacity to make every line so significant that it revealed a specific trait of the person he was depicting. There are many moods expressed in the numerous caricatures he left, and some of his sketches are bitingly satirical; but as a rule Caruso stressed the broad, human side of his subjects. By far the greatest number of his drawings concern themselves with the comic aspect of frail humanity, and in the many humorous sketches of himself Caruso laughed as heartily—if not more heartily—at his own frailties as he laughed at the frailties of his friends or of contemporary notables in art and politics or of the anonymous subjects that caught his clear eye.

The character sketches Caruso drew of four ex-presidents of the United States—Grover Cleveland, Theodore Roosevelt, William H. Taft, and Woodrow Wilson—show how completely he had grasped the salient traits of

each man; he was both kind and just. His
Kaiser Wilhelm is a masterpiece, and the
gruesome iron mask, the very soul of the man
back of it, is truly a stroke of genius. It is
remarkable that whomever he chose to portray
—whether Alfonso XIII of Spain, Nicholas
II of Russia, Edward VII of England, or
even Mohammed V, Sultan of Turkey, or
Hamed Mizza, Shah of Persia—Caruso never
failed to give us a vivid presentation, extremely different as all these personalities
were. Mere draftsmanship could never have
achieved such feats of character-drawing;
there was the same keen intelligence, the same
remarkable understanding of human nature,
directing the practiced skill of his pencil that
directed his interpretations of operatic rôles.

In his drawings of his friends and of his
colleagues at the Metropolitan Opera House,
Caruso was lavish with his overbubbling
humor. Signor Gatti-Casazza must have discovered many an amusing streak in his own
character, unknown to him before, when he
gazed on some of the delightful sketches Caruso made of him. Caruso's old and devoted
friend, Antonio Scotti, must frequently have

laughed as he looked at the humorous contortions the great tenor put him into. Nor did Caruso neglect the fair prima donnas of the Metropolitan. Madame Farrar, Madame Sembrich, Madame Alda, Madame Eames— Caruso was very daring, indeed, when he closed his eyes to their irresistible charms in order to record their foibles. The conductors are all represented, too, in that remarkable collection of caricatures. Mahler, Campanini, and Toscanini are caught in their most characteristic moments. Nor did he neglect his favorite composers. He made very striking character sketches of Verdi, Saint-Saëns, Charpentier, Leoncavallo, and Mascagni.

Caruso's great skill in his avocation, then, was overshadowed only by his greater skill in his vocation. American newspapers were quick, however, to see the value of Caruso's second art, and one editor once offered him large sums to draw exclusively for his paper. But Caruso replied: "I make enough money singing."

In the summer of 1920 he spent some of his leisure in modeling a striking head of himself as Eléazar in "La Juive," and said that it was the first time in ten years that he had done any modeling in clay. His last previous effort in this branch of his avocation had been the wonderful bronze caricature of himself which he kept on his piano. Enrico Caruso was certainly blessed by more than one fairy!

A man of many hobbies, once Caruso took to something he pursued it with enthusiasm. At one time he became interested in rare old coins, and before much water had flowed under bridges he was an ardent collector. His particular interest attached itself to ancient Roman, Italian, and American gold coins. Within a comparatively brief period he had succeeded in amassing a large and valuable collection, which included many of the rarer American gold pieces—old California issues such as the 1851 California $50 octagonal gold slug, issued to commemorate the gold craze, and the oblong Köhler California $20 gold piece of 1850. When he bought the two silver dollars called "Gloria" and "Metrica," issued in 1897, Caruso was delighted to find that one of them bore the name of his little daughter.

Another hobby was composition, or perhaps

—for Caruso made no pretensions to being a composer—it should be called melodic invention. He was accustomed to read a great number of new songs with me, and going over them we would select such as might seem worth while studying for one purpose or another. Sometimes he would invent a melody himself, and he had a real gift for finding a tuneful air of a lyric character which lent itself easily and naturally to a good harmonic background. Various of these songs have been published and have won favor. He also gave generous encouragement to those of his friends who composed, and he had sung a song of my own, "Soltanto a te," which I wrote for him, a number of times in concert, and had even made a record of it—which has not as yet been issued—before his last illness.

But the birth of his daughter Gloria cast all his other hobbies in the shade, and even his beloved caricatures held only a secondary interest for Caruso after her advent. The cradle songs he sang her would have earned him thousands of dollars on the stage, for like the artist he was, he sang as well for her at home as for any audience at the opera.

Some one once said of Caruso: "The Old World gave him fame, the New World an income." This, of course, is not exactly true. The New World, in particular the United States, gave him more than anything else, something which Caruso warmly appreciated: it gave him sympathy, understanding, affection. It adopted him as one of its national characters; it made him an American. He came to regard the United States as his home, and it was in New York that he gave his hostages to fortune and took his chief joy in the daughter presented to him by his American wife. It is perhaps for these reasons, for all that they are uncommercial, that Caruso's European appearances tended, as the years passed, to become more and more incidental. It was not that he loved Europe less, possibly, but that he loved America more.

The details of Enrico Caruso's illness, apparent recovery, and unexpected death are but too well known. On the evening of November 30, 1920, while he was singing the rôle of Samson at the Metropolitan, a descending pillar of the scenes injured his head; at

the "Pagliacci" performance of December 8,
he severely strained his side in his exit; on
December 12, in "L'Elisir d'Amore" at the
Brooklyn Academy of Music, he burst a
minor blood vessel in his throat. He spent
Sunday quietly in bed, and his condition so
improved that he sang in "La Forza del Destino" at the Metropolitan on Monday night,
with wonderful virility and buoyancy of voice.
But a performance of "La Juive" on December 24 was his last and supreme effort.

Following two operations—his illness was
diagnosed as pleurisy—he seemed for a time
to be well on the road to recovery, when, on
February 16, he suffered a serious relapse.
His son, Enrico, Jr., attending a military
school in Culver, Ind., was summoned to his
bedside, oxygen was administered, and the
last rites of the Roman Church were given
him at midnight. Great throngs crowded
about the bulletin boards; wires and cables
arrived from all parts of the world; and the
President of the United States called up from
Washington on the long distance telephone to
inquire as to his condition. His will to live
triumphed, and by March 1 he was able to

stand a minor operation. In April he could walk about his room without the aid of a cane, and on May 28 he sailed for Naples for a complete rest, expecting to return in the fall and resume his work at the Metropolitan.

A week before his death at the Hotel Vesuvius, on August 2—he had been living quietly in Naples, making short trips, and taking sun-baths—he had tried his voice, and his friends found it held all the golden melody and sonorous power which had marked it before his illness. He had made a vow in New York that, if he recovered his voice, he would undertake a pilgrimage to the shrine of the Madonna of Pompeii, and he now felt that the time to fulfil his vow had arrived. After his visit to the shrine, he imprudently examined the excavations, and caught a cold which settled in his stomach. The specialists called to attend him found that he was suffering from a subphrenic abscess accompanied by severe peritonitis, and all their efforts to save his life proved unavailing.

The flood of tributes and appreciations which his death called forth in the press of every land eloquently testified to the unique place he held in the general estimation. The great artists who were his colleagues, his intimate friends, the thousands who had enjoyed his glorious gift of song were united in a common grief. His art was international—for all that New York considered him peculiarly her own—and the whole world mourned an irreparable loss in his passing. On the morning of August 4, a requiem mass was celebrated in the Church of San Francesco di Paolo in Naples, and in the afternoon his body was removed in solemn processional. His obsequies were royal. Had he been able to see through the crystal of his casket, he could have realized the love and fidelity of his compatriots. The Queen of England and his friends in New York had supplied the flowers heaped on the hearse, which was drawn through the streets by six horses, an aeroplane escorting it in the skies, while cordons of soldiers of the Italian army paid military honors to the cortège, and held back the immense throngs who crowded the square. Speeches were made by the Prefect of Naples as the representative of the King of Italy and the Government, and by others, and then the hearse proceeded slowly from the Piazza del Plebiscito to the temporary resting-place of the body in the vault of the Canessa family, pending the finishing of the monument, to be executed by Cifariello, which will complete the great tenor's own vault.

Caruso's voice—authentically the greatest of its period—has departed, save for that near approach to its original beauty which is preserved in the numerous phonograph records he made and which will not allow it to be forgotten—as the voices of so many other great artists have been forgotten—even when the generations who heard Caruso himself sing have passed away. But the lesson of his art remains—his guiding rules, his exercises, his own precept and practice for the development of the singing voice. As one who was for years his friend and accompanist, one who knew his generosity and liberality of spirit as well as his daily routine of voice study and development, I feel that he would be the first to commend my present endeavor to place at the disposal of every student of singing those lessons which his own study of the art of song has placed at my disposal. It would make him happy to know that others might derive benefit from the results of his own experience, and that the truths of voice training and voice development which he learned as the result of years of hard and intensive work, might serve to lead others along the paths he himself trod.

Chapter VI

THE SECRET OF CARUSO'S GREAT
BREATHING POWER

Caruso moved the hearts of his myriad hearers in so direct and compelling a manner that they accepted his wonderful art as a spontaneous, natural outburst of song, which did not require a directing intelligence. The vast multitudes who listened to him were completely carried away by that luscious voice, whose tones seemed to come from another world; they were overpowered by an utterance that ravished their ears without revealing the effort and art involved in its production.

Caruso, like every true artist, felt intensely. But it was the consummate art with which he expressed his deep feeling that enabled him to stir his hearers as few singers have ever done. For back of the deep feeling there was deep reflection; his mind was always in full control of his emotions. Even musicians often overlooked the great rôle Caruso's mind played in the development and perfecting of his art, although the fact is that his marvelous voice itself was to a great extent the product of ceaseless and untiring observation and analysis, as well as of constant search for means of improving his mastery of the organs with which nature had endowed him.

There are still a few intimates who remember that Caruso began with a voice which was by no means the miracle that for more than a quarter of a century packed the opera houses of New York, Buenos Aires, Havana, and Mexico, to say nothing of occasional engagements in London, Berlin, Paris, and elsewhere on the Continent. The miracle to which we are now referring is the phenomenal vocal capacity which even the public that recognized the wide scope of his song art took for granted. It cannot be doubted, of course, that Caruso had been provided by nature with a remarkable vocal instrument and with a powerful pair of bellows; nevertheless we know from our long association with the great artist—and Caruso himself often expressed his own conviction of the fact—that it was his genius for work which made the utmost of his endowment both as regards the physical organs and those native emotional and mental resources upon which his final artistry drew so heavily. Work does not mean unguided labor: nothing could be more ruinous to the vocal organism. To the genuine artist work can only mean intelligent direction, painstaking study, and infinite patience. These are the quintessential elements in any enduring success.

From the physiological point of view, the larynx, the pharynx, the mouth chamber, the nasal passages, together with the trachea (windpipe) and lungs, form the organs of respiration, and at the same time are called upon for the production and perfect rendering of tones, thus constituting the vocal organs. This machinery is to be found in every human body, with a conformation more or less favorable to the production of tone; but into Caruso's body nature had marvelously introduced an amazingly equal perfection of each of the vocal organs, with the result that no human voice has been able to produce tones of greater richness and poignancy. The diameter of Caruso's larynx as a vocal organ

accorded so precisely with the diameter required for its functioning as an organ of respiration that, while its singing function admirably served the upper ranges of his voice,
the breathing function bestowed upon him
those ample, rich, and powerful tones. The
lateral amplitude of his larynx, by permitting
a maximum dilation of the glottis, accounted
for extraordinary respiratory powers.

Enrico Caruso's unusual vocal mechanism
was certainly the medium which enabled him
to achieve his complete mastery of the difficult art of singing; without this physical endowment he would not perhaps have attained
his unrivaled position in the world of pure
song. On the other hand, had Caruso failed
to use these marvelous organs correctly, intelligently, we can say unhesitatingly that he
would have gone the way of many another
obscure singer of strong physique blessed with
a remarkable instrument—after a brief period
in the limelight, a sudden banishment to the
land of disappointed tenors. A telling point
to recall in this connection is that among the
students of the *Scuola Vergine*—where Caruso received his first serious vocal training—

he was known as *il tenore vento,* a name that
hardly suggests richness of tone production
or grandeur of style. On the contrary it suggests that Caruso's greatness was due as much
to his correct and intelligent use of his vocal
organs as to the actual possession of them.

Because Enrico Caruso knew that the
breath is the motive power of the voice, for it
is the action of the breath upon the vocal organs which brings about the production of
tone—and, therefore, pitch and musical phrasing as well as tone production fundamentally
depend on the breath—he devoted a great deal
of study and thought to this the groundwork
of his art. It must not be thought, however,
that he speculated about and labored over fantastic theories which promised overnight phenomenal results. Caruso believed in the gospel of work—not mere labor, but intelligent
work—the mainspring of enduring achievement; and he severely condemned meretricious
nostrums that purport to lead to rapid success.
He knew full well what effort and thought it
had cost him, what unsparing pains and patience, to master completely the control of his

breath, without which all his other great gifts or attainments would have been of no avail.

All who are interested in the art of singing know the troubles young singers—and often those already engaged in concert and opera work—meet in their search for a correct method of breathing. In their wanderings from one maestro to another they are sometimes told to breathe naturally and the breath will take care of itself. They set to work breathing as naturally as nature will allow them and find this "method" excellent for their daily speech; but once they begin to sing, a cramped feeling comes upon them, their tone production is poor, their phrasing choppy, and ofttimes they struggle desperately to stick to pitch. All these troubles seem to be the result of lack of motive power, of a gasping for breath. It is evident that their "natural method" did not help them very considerably.

Now what was the secret of Caruso's great breathing power? What method of breathing —for we have seen that some method for managing the breath is essential—did Caruso invoke that he should have enjoyed such ample reserves of breath? Caruso employed (and perhaps rediscovered) the method which the great Italian masters of bel canto had taught: he drew in, retained, and exhaled his breath in a mode different in no way from the manner always prescribed by the masters of beautiful singing—*diaphragmatic intercostal breathing.* We use the words *diaphragmatic* and *intercostal* advisedly: in the normal human body the diaphragmatic and costal methods of breathing are always used together, the one assisting and supplementing the other.

During Enrico Caruso's artistic career there were many would-be singers who besieged him for an opinion or some advice regarding their voice or their system of singing. I would be called in to examine them, and hence would hear many interesting expositions and dissertations, in the course of which Caruso ably demonstrated that for a singer there can be only one effective mode of breathing. As a matter of fact, all these students had either pursued a bad system of respiration, in so far as singing is concerned, or had practiced their system incorrectly, and consequently had failed to obtain a long and well-regulated air pressure, without which there can be no good tone production or vocal mastery.

Caruso always addressed those who sought the mysterious secret of his breathing power in some such words as these:

"I perform the act of respiration or breathing just as you do, with only two movements, namely, inspiration and expiration, which means the drawing in and the letting out of the breath."

Whereupon Caruso, without any stiffness, would place his body in an erect position, with one foot a bit in advance of the other, as if to take a step. (It is important to note here that his entire body was completely relaxed— no portion of it rigid.) Then he would slightly contract (draw in) the muscles of the abdomen and inhale calmly and without haste. As a result of this deep and slow inspiration of air, his diaphragm and ribs would expand and his thorax (chest) rise. At this point of the demonstration Caruso always called the student's attention especially to the diaphragm, explaining that when it assumed this position it constituted the principal agent for sustaining the column of air which could be held in the lungs under the pressure required for the production of loud or soft tones.

"The second movement is exhalation."

Here Caruso would perform certain vocal exercises, of which I reproduce below the one most frequently used by him.

EXERCISE I

Caruso would sing all the above exercise during his second movement, that of expiration, carefully emitting the air inhaled during the first movement—without any straining, but with the least possible rapidity—in the volume required for the correct rendering of this exercise.[1] At the end of the exercise, his thorax, diaphragm, and abdomen returned to their original positions.

The exercise practiced by Caruso had developed the muscles of his diaphragm to such

[1] Exercise VI (in the chapter on tone production) illustrates the manner in which Exercise I should be sung.

a degree that he was wont to give those students who came to him a little demonstration of his power. He would have them press a closed fist with all their strength against his relaxed diaphragm; then suddenly, through a voluntary contraction of his diaphragm, he would violently fling off that pressure of the fist.

There is one other factor, indeed highly important, which we must stress in connection with Caruso's great breathing power—the mental factor. Caruso could inhale slowly and steadily so ample a breath that he was able to exhale at very great length, not only because the physiological process of expiration is longer than that of inspiration, but also because Caruso had succeeded in adding to his auto-physiological control the volitional control which comes from the brain. By dint of a vigilant mental effort—though, always without any physical strain—Caruso governed the expiratory flow of the breath with such mastery that not a particle of it escaped without giving up its necessary equivalent in tone. Besides, Caruso emitted for each musical phrase, or even for each note, just enough breath to produce that phrase or note musically, and no more. The remainder of his breath he kept in reserve, which made the enchanted hearer feel that the master was still far from the limit of his resources, that he had retained ample motive power for whatever the occasion should require. That is the revealing sign of all great art and it is, in a manner of speech, the bedrock of all great singing.

Therefore, the secret of Caruso's priceless gift, his great capacity for respiration, although partly due to the amazing perfection of his vocal apparatus, was also, and perhaps mainly, due to his power of concentration upon the study of himself and of the natural means at his disposition. This ability in Caruso—the power to transform every particle of breath into tone and the power to control the breath so that no more of it need be used for the good production of a note or phrase than was absolutely essential—should be the goal of every singer. In fact, we believe we can justly say that without this principle there can be no great singing.

Enrico Caruso strongly advised the student, in respiration exercises, to practice breathing

through the nose and through the mouth at the
same time, although one should depend chiefly
upon inhaling through the nose, because that
is the more spontaneous and the more natural,
as well as the more effective, method. In any
case, the act of inhalation should be visible to
a spectator solely through the raising of the
thorax, and not, after the practice of many
misguided singers, through the lifting of the
shoulders. This latter movement the singer
would never be obliged to make were he to
use the intercostal diaphragmatic method of
respiration.

This method, moreover, enabled Caruso to
keep his organs of respiration sound and
armored them against all weaknesses. At the
same time, thanks to the aid of his mental control, he was never at a loss to sustain to the
end a lengthy musical phrase, was never under
the necessity of cutting it short or of finishing it off pitch or by a forced prolongation.

The foregoing discussion should be sufficient
to demonstrate that the singer must not put
his principal dependence on any other type
of respiration—on, for instance, either the
clavicular or the abdominal. Whenever one

exerts himself violently he breathes violently;
as a result his collar-bone or clavicle is for-
cibly drawn up by the muscles of the neck in
order to assist the action of the intercostal
muscles, which act on the ribs. This is the
method of breathing known as the clavicular.
It is always a partial respiration; and besides
being used during very violent exertion, it is
also resorted to in certain diseased states of
the body. Furthermore, in order to succeed
in realizing its full power, one must give his
hands a firm grasp on some fixed object.
That is why the unhappy singer who resorts
to the vicious clavicular method of respiration
seeks, whenever he can, to lay hold of something solid—so violent is the effort he makes.
He is a sad spectacle indeed, his head thrown
back or thrust forward, his face flushed, his
whole body rigid, his outstretched arms begging for the breath that fails to come. Imagine the tone production of a singer who is
laboring under so great a physical strain! In
such circumstances any artistic rendering of a
musical phrase is too much to expect: the un-
fortunate performer may, thanks to his sad
plight, arouse the sympathy of his hearers;

he certainly will not move them musically by so painful an art.

Whenever Enrico Caruso witnessed the torture such singers inflict on themselves, though he never failed of sympathy for the victim, he was unequivocal in his condemnation of the method. He would exclaim: "Why, the poor fellow is violating the first principle of art— the concealment of the artist's effort. Why doesn't he learn how to breathe? It is impossible to sing artistically without a thorough mastery of breath control. Why don't singers stop to think, and work intelligently? They would soon realize that all great art is the product of reserve, restraint; without these, vocal technique is imperfect, and imperfect technique means imperfect art."

The abdominal method of breathing, or the method that draws most of its force from the abdominal muscles, is ineffective, both because it constitutes a relaxation of the visceral organs, and also—and this is the chief objection—because the diaphragm receives no support in the act of expiration. With the diaphragm unsupported, it is more difficult to control the emission of the air from the lungs.

Furthermore, in relying chiefly on his abdominal muscles for inspiration, the singer cannot fill his lungs to their full capacity.

The aim in any search for a method of breathing is twofold: first, the most effective manner of getting the lungs completely full of air, which is the motive power of singing; secondly, the most effective manner of controlling the emission of the air from the lungs so that every particle shall be transformed into tone. In both of these processes Enrico Caruso was able to achieve phenomenal success because he employed the intercostal diaphragmatic method of respiration, but it must not be forgotten that to his sound method he brought a high degree of mental concentration, which kept his powerful bellows under complete control.

For the control of the breath, Caruso practiced the following exercise—running the whole chromatic scale up to C, and sometimes up to C sharp—in one single sustained breath.

EXERCISE II [1]

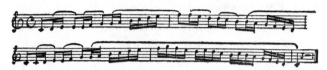

[1] These exercises as well as the others which will follow are also useful for the purpose of increasing the agility and flexibility of the vocal organs.

CHAPTER VII

TONE PRODUCTION

1

TONE ATTACK

In the preceding chapter we endeavored to get at the source of Caruso's great breathing power. We observed that, remarkable as was the vigor of his constitution, the final secret of his wonderful breath control lay in his intelligent management of his respiration. His manner of inhalation, to be sure, supplied him with ample motive power; but this reservoir of power would have been of indifferent effect had he failed to make use of every particle of the outgoing column of air. It was this perfect control over the emission of breath, so that no air should be exhaled unproductively, that enabled Caruso to attain his unique mastery of tone production.

A good tone production, of course, must take account of other essential elements. There must be relaxation, for instance, a complete absence of strain of any sort. But the one indispensable condition, the principle which can never be disregarded without making the tone unsatisfactory, is the rule that the emission of the singer's breath and the attack of the tone must take place simultaneously. This is the first secret of a beautiful, round, musical tone. Should the singer allow any air to escape before he attacks the tone, then the result will be a breathy sound, ragged and disagreeable. Furthermore, once the attack or beginning is poor, the rest of the tone will be harsh and unpleasant, or at best it will be veiled or cloudy.

As regards the connection between breathing and tone attack, a great deal has been written about the *cupa di glotta, coup de glotte,* or stroke of the glottis. This device may be described simply as a clucking sound produced by the forceful contact of the air column against the closed vocal chords. In order to bring such a contact about, the singer is requested to act exactly as if he were to utter a slight cough. It is the audible stroke of the glottis, and it is supposed to prevent the singer from emitting air before the tone is attacked. If by this means the singer does succeed in controlling his breath, so that he achieves a crisp, decisive attack, he also succeeds in producing a hard, metallic tone that is cold and repellent. Not only is this explosive tone attack objectionable on æsthetic grounds, but also it is in the long run injurious to the vocal organs. It is always an unnatural method; and all essentially unnatural methods, besides producing unnatural sounds, tend to impair the proper functioning of the natural organs.

Now, Caruso had a perfect tone attack. In his ravishing outpour of song all the tones, clean and clear at their inception, continued mellow and rich, coming forth from his glorious instrument with a warm and captivating glow. If he made use of this famous stroke of the glottis, he certainly employed it in a modified form and in the most moderate manner, taking pains in all cantilena singing to avoid the unnatural explosive effect which does much to destroy the appealing quality of a tone. Here again we may say without hesitance that Caruso obtained his superb results in the matter of tone attack through his habitual perseverance in the method of intelligent experimentation and study. He was almost unmercifully critical of himself, perpetually on the watch for possible flaws; nor was he ever satisfied with his work until his exacting ear had given him its approval.

In his tone attack Caruso succeeded in coordinating into one act the flying together of the vocal chords and the emission of the breath. The two movements coincided so precisely that there was never any effort, any strain or forcing back of this act. He breathed with great ease, and he strove to produce his tones with the same ease. It is a skill which is extremely difficult to achieve; but this way lies the road of great singing.

It must not be thought that we are attempting to set down rigid rules, drawn from Caruso's art and so codified that they may be servilely followed by everybody. Caruso, there is no doubting, would have been the first to condemn strongly such a procedure. He always contended that every individual is provided with a distinct vocal instrument, and that every instrument demands and deserves distinct and intelligent care in its cultivation.

The great tenor was much too genuine an
artist to let himself be hampered by the dog-
matic precepts formulated by theorists, many
of whom, unfortunately, know little of the
singer's art. He had no use at all for vague
and incomprehensible theories. In fact, so individual a matter did Caruso consider his art
that he would often question the value of any
method that seemed too generally applied.
The singer, like every other artist, must take
for his first and foremost study his own
vehicle of expression—the vocal organs nature has provided him with—and thus essay
to discover what are his proper vocal resources.
Caruso did exactly this. He studied his vocal
apparatus, his vocal capacity, and his temperament; these he sought to develop to their
full power and utmost perfection. At the
same time he took infinite care—and in this
fact very probably lies the fundamental secret
of Caruso's art—not to abuse, by any sort of
strain or forcing, the gifts nature had bestowed on him.

We know that Caruso, even in his great
moments, never forced his breath in an effort
to gain more power. It is equally true of his

tone production. How to turn all of the motive power of his breath into pure tone without straining his vocal organs—that was the quintessential problem for Caruso. And here again he had recourse to his thorough knowledge of his vocal instrument, a hard won knowledge which was at once so detailed and so precise that it enabled him to achieve a tone control adequate to render all the gradations, inflections, and nuances of which the human voice is capable.

2

TONE FORMATION

On the subject of the natural means which aid and favor a good emission of tone, Caruso expressed himself as follows:

"For a good production of tone there are two elements to be considered; the first element is *internal,* the second *external.* The internal element concerns the muscles of the throat, which act in sympathy with the facial muscles; the external concerns the position which our body assumes while the tone is being emitted. It is necessary, therefore, through the aid of self-study and the help of a good singing teacher, to become aware of every physical defect—such as contractions of the muscles of the throat, of the face, or of the jaw—which can hinder the tone from being emitted in all its fullness and purity. These rigid muscular contractions bring about a throaty tone, which lacks support and is incapable of purity and amplitude.

"In the second place, one must take into consideration the defects which are external and consequently visible. A discomposed movement of the body, an exaggerated raising of the head while singing, or a too studied position of the chest will always interfere with the free emission of the tone, especially in a student whose self-mastery is still limited.

"The singer should apply himself to his study with great naturalness and relaxation: this is the *sine qua non* of beautiful cantilena singing. When he is exercising his voice he must not disturb the composure of his face, because every contraction of the face is reflected in the throat. A contracted face indicates a lack of composure; whereas it is essential that the singer should bring to his vocal study a complete calmness. Unless he is calm, how can he hope to control his will? Moreover, a calm mind facilitates the task of completely relaxing the vocal organs."

It is evident that in making these remarks Caruso had in mind the practicing of *vocalizzi*, or vocalises as they are called in English— exercises or passages to be vocalized. And there is no more valuable practice for beginners or even for singers already a good way along the road of vocal art. By vocalization is meant singing upon vowels and not upon words—whether upon one or more vowels or upon one or a series of notes, does not matter. It is only one part of the operation of utterance, for it does not involve articulation. Now, pure vocalization is obtained by bringing into play those muscles of the vocal organism—*and no others*—which are essential to the production of the vowel at the moment being sung. Though the action of the unnecessary muscles might not destroy the actual vowel sound, it would destroy the possibility of good tone production—the quality of the tone thus emitted is usually "throaty" or "veiled." All this evil the misguided singer brings down on his head the moment he attempts to gain power by forcing or straining his vocal organs. This evil is by no means peculiarly characteristic of poor singers; poor pianists and poor violinists also frequently attempt to strain and force their resources in an effort to gain more power than nature has put at their disposal. For them, however, the pernicious procedure is not so dangerous; they can be corrected by a good master before any real harm has been visited upon their fingers or their wrists. It is not so with the singer. The vocal organism is too delicate an instrument to endure a great deal of strain or forcing, and the penalty for even a little abuse of this kind is a "cracked" voice.

Caruso, then, did not force his tone production, as tenors unfortunately are wont to do; as a consequence he emitted tones that were always pure and of a harmonious and compelling beauty. So much for his production of single tones. When he vocalized on a passage or on a series of tones, whether at a slow or a rapid tempo, he always sought to do it with the same ease with which he emitted one tone. In progressing from one tone to another he did not change the sound of the vowel sung or the quality of the production. At the same time he permitted none of his breath to escape unproductively, that is, between one tone and the other,—the secret of pure legato singing.

The factors which enter into the production of a tone vary according to its pitch, its intensity—that is to say, its volume—or its timbre. Some of these factors, of course, the singer consciously manipulates and controls: they have to do with such matters as the air-blast, the position of the head and of the tongue, the shaping of the mouth, and so on. But there are other factors—as, notably, the tension and relaxation of the vocal chords in the regulation of pitch—which are brought into play unconsciously and can be guided by nothing except the singer's tone perception.

By pitch is meant the degree of acuteness or of graveness in a tone, the degree being determined by the number of vibrations (per second) that produce it; the greater the number of vibrations the higher the pitch of the tone, the fewer the number of vibrations the lower the pitch of the tone. It is of primal importance for the singer, as for all musicians, that he have a keen perception of pitch. Indeed, this faculty, which is customarily referred to as his "ear," is almost a separate sense; for it is in very large measure innate, a natural endowment which, like the memory, can be cultivated but cannot be created where there is no instinctive foundation upon which to build. If it can be cultivated, however, it can also be ruined. Slovenly practice has blunted the ear of many a student and has rapidly taken from him whatever natural perception of pitch he may originally have had. It is therefore essential that he practice slowly and with great care, so that he may give his special attention to the precision in pitch of his tones. They may be as heavenly as the human voice can make them, but let their pitch be faulty and they will be unbearable.

The homogeneous fixity of Caruso's vocal tones was truly marvelous. The vibrations of each tone he emitted continued uninterrupted and unaltered throughout its entire duration and suffered no perceptible disturbance from secondary sounds. Caruso possessed a fine ear, and his pitch perception was unusually keen. We cannot recall a single occasion when his intonation was not absolutely pure. There were times when, owing to some indisposition, his voice was "off color," when his tones failed to come forth with their usual magical beauty of quality; but there was never a time when they were off pitch.

For his precision of intonation he could, once more, bestow part of his thanks on his remarkable breath control, since breathing is naturally a great factor in the regulation of pitch; but however accurate the ear with which he began, and however great the assistance given by his breath control, it was the infinite pains and care with which Caruso practiced that made him the master of pitch as it made him the master of the other phases of the vocal art. There can be no art without talent, but it is intelligent, painstaking, and persevering practice that makes perfect art.

EXERCISE III

Caruso at times used the above exercise for the perfecting of precision of pitch. It is also excellent for the blending of the vowels and the mastery of the breath control.

The intensity of a tone is the power or energy with which it is produced. Intensity is the basis of nuance and dynamics in vocal art; without it, singing becomes deadly monotonous and ceases to be an art. Accordingly it is of vital importance for the singer to comprehend thoroughly what regulates the various degrees of intensity in a tone. Here again the principal part is played by the motive power, the column of air which is supplied by the lungs. The singer can scarcely aspire to control the intensity of his tone unless he has learned how to control his breath. And by the same sign, in order to develop the intensity of his tone, he must develop his breath power. The singer can never escape from the motor of the vocal artist—the breath.

It is at once most interesting and most encouraging to know how gradual was the development of Caruso's vocal organs. His first serious teacher, Guglielmo Vergine, though he recognized that Caruso possessed a fine instrument, never suspected to what a richness and power this voice, which was then rather thin, could finally be developed. We have already taken note of the fact that the students of Vergine looked upon their fellow pupil as a *tenore vento*—a thin, reedy tenor. So we must recognize as irresistible the natural conclusion that Caruso's development, even though it enjoyed the initial advantage of the very exceptional anatomic qualities of his vocal organs, attained its ultimate perfection through the practice of vocal exercises under the guidance of a wise system. Moreover, it should be noted that in Caruso's case the development of intensity was constant and progressive: starting as a *tenore vento,* he revealed himself, first as a lyric tenor, and then as a dramatic tenor—and a real one. We say a real one because, unlike innumerable singers who are possessed by the dramatic ambition, Caruso had the ability to attain his ambition, not only through his method of interpretation but also through the genuine energy and power of the vocal resources he had built up.

The following two exercises Caruso used for developing the intensity of tone production.

EXERCISE IV

EXERCISE V

After pitch and intensity we have to consider, as the third element in tone production, the matter of timbre. Timbre is the quality of the tone produced.

If Buffon was at all justified in his celebrated phrase, that style is the man himself, we may say that timbre is the singer himself. Of vocal artists, in particular, is it true that the quality of the tone each makes is the quality of the artist; for there is nothing in which singers differ so widely from one another as in the quality of their voices.

At first glance this looks surprising. Other musicians employ widely varying techniques to draw their characteristic tones from their instruments which may be good, bad, or indifferent in their manufacture. One would expect to find violinists, pianists, or even performers on such standardized instruments as those of the tympani family producing a greater gamut of timbres than are possible to singers, who make their tones inside themselves. Here the basis of tone quality, far from being a matter of skillful or clumsy manufacture of instruments out of a profusion of fine or coarse materials, is at bottom a physical condition. Vocal tone must depend considerably on the general vocal organism with which nature has provided the singer. The anatomical cause for varying timbre in the voice is merely the varying adaptation of the position of the resonance cavities to the functions of the glottis.

A violin may be a Cremona, a Stradivarius, or the machine turned, varnish-laden child of a furniture factory consecrated to nothing finer than quantity production; a piano may be built by artists for the fingers of a master or assembled by day laborers for the instalation of a mechanical player; but human beings are human beings, and throats are throats. This fact would seem, at first glance, to set narrower limits to the range of vocal timbres.

Yet we know the reverse to be the case. Voices differ as no hand-made instruments can. And not only is there a variety of the comparatively simple physical instruments nature bestows on singers, but it is also true that artistic control and wise manipulation of the vocal resonators can alter the tone quality or color of a given voice by such fine gradations as to make it almost a series of instruments.

Caruso, for instance, was able to bring those resonant vocal organs from which issued his extensive, rich, and powerful voice so completely under the control of his will that the slightest modification in the movement of his lips and cheeks, accompanying the swiftest transition in the emotions and passions represented, gave him tones of infinite color and of inexhaustible, of ever-renascent melodious beauty. This is the way in which the vocal artist makes the timbre of his voice the vehicle for his musical personality. The man is the voice, but he is more than the vocal instrument he received at birth: he is the master of all his vocal resources.

We can only speculate as to what another singer—less intelligent, less self-critical, less persevering—might have made of Caruso's natal equipment: what we can know beyond cavil is that it was Caruso's mastery of this equipment which produced tone colors so finely wrought, and spread over so wide a range of delicate nuances, that he was unexcelled, and became unique, in the world of song. This is the real reason why his voice continues to survive, as if in the spirit, within the minds of all who heard it, although his physical instrument has been silenced forever.

3

REGISTERS OF THE VOICE

Speaking generally, the nomenclature employed in the vocal art is so vague as to be inadequate for exact denotation. A good part of the vagueness rises from a certain habit of naming vocal divisions on subjective rather than objective grounds, or rather, of determining class names by physical sensations more or less peculiar to the namer. We now approach a problem where this observation is particularly pertinent—the complex questions of the registers of the voice.

The register of a voice is its compass. Various singing masters and singers have variously divided the vocal compass into sections representing, or purporting to represent, the different registers which demand different physical methods for their execution. To a very large degree, however, these systems of division have been theoretical and inexact, for the reason that nearly all of them have been based on the theorists' own physical sensations without due regard to the actual facts. Such arbitrary systems are not redeemed by the fact that they are always more or less supported by vague physiological hypotheses.

Nevertheless, the question of registers is of utmost importance to the singer, for, since it involves the problem of equalizing the voice, it must be intimately connected with tone production. One highly significant fact most of the theorists, obsessed as they have been by their fanciful notions, have failed to understand. Whether there are two, three, five, or seven registers; whether the artist sings in the lower, middle, or upper range of his vocal compass; he must needs bear in mind one all-important principle: his tone production must be sound throughout, and every note he sings must be beautiful. Let the singer take heed to apply intelligently the principles that make for good tone production and the question of registers will afford him little worry.

Caruso never let the complicated and thankless matter of registers disturb him. He knew that there was only one vital goal to strive for —the production of beautiful tones. On this goal he focused all his musical intelligence; toward it he concentrated all his mental and spiritual energy.

It is strange indeed that so many moderns should have gone astray in this matter of registers. The early Italian singing masters had already penetrated the subject with admirable insight. Those old masters had the good sense to keep in plain view the one significant object—beautiful singing. They did not put the cart before the horse by theorizing before they experimented. They did not force arbitrary, preconceived notions on their pupils. On the contrary, they were guided in their formulating of vocal principles by the achievements of the great vocal artists of their time.

The singing masters of the past recognized two registers, which they described as *voce piena* and *voce finta*—that is *full voice* and *feigned (artificial, disguised) voice.* These are the two registers which are at present so often described as "chest voice" (or "chest tones") and "head voice" (or "head tones"). The head tones are also sometimes referred to as "falsetto tones." The so-called "chest tones" are often subdivided, for the sake of convenience, into "lower" and "medium" registers. Any further classification of registers, whatever its appeal to the theorist, can be of no practical benefit to the student, and it can easily confuse him at a time when his whole attention should be concentrated on tone production, to the exclusion of scientific, and pseudo-scientific divisions of the scale.

If the behavior of the singer's vocal membranes knows any change at all throughout the entire range of his voice, it takes place when he passes from the chest register to that

of the head. In the case of the voice that has
been badly trained, or has not been trained
at all, the change in the physical process of
tone production is invariably accompanied by
a sensation of straining and of tension in the
larynx and its adjacent parts. The real
singer, the one who has had a good schooling,
is revealed precisely by the evenness and
facility with which he passes from one register
to the other. Once more the vocal artist must
remember that he does not sing *with* his
throat but *through* it; that tone is produced
by the breath, the vocal motor, as it comes into
contact with the vocal chords; and that the
other vocal organs, acting as resonators,
merely vary the quality of the tone. Careful
breath control, the *sine qua non* of beautiful
singing, will help him considerably over the
thorny road of equalizing his entire vocal
range.

When the tones are fed and properly supported by a column of air under complete control; and, furthermore, when due precaution
is taken that there be no strain or forcing in
the production; then the voice attains throughout its range a beautiful equality which all

but makes even the theorizing listener forget the very existence of his precious registers. In this respect Caruso had so thorough and artistic a command of voice, so perfect an equalization from one extremity to the other of his tremendous vocal compass, that all the problems surrounding the dispute about the registers were conspicuous only in their significant absence. Yet it must never be thought that Caruso's apparent ease, the seemingly natural perfection of his production, was arrived at by a short cut, or over no road at all. The *laissez-faire* method in voice culture was anathema to him, and we have long since seen the overwhelming evidence that he was led to his shining success in the vocal art by a guiding intelligence which never relaxed its alertness throughout his long career. What, then, was the secret of that smooth and even production, so suave in its perfection and so natural in its execution that the listener was always tempted to think it miraculous? The best answer is in his own words.

"The vocal range of a singer," Caruso would say, "must be built up by degrees and with infinite care. The purity and ease of production in the upper range depend to a great extent on the manner in which the lower tones leading up to it are sung. If the lower tones are produced correctly, and an even poise is maintained in ascending the scale the higher tones will benefit by the support of the lower ones—especially by keeping the throat well open—and thus avoid the pinching quality often present in the highest tones of a singer's range."

Nor was Caruso ever an advocate of the thread-like tone, unsupported by plenty of breath and taken with the so-called "head voice." It is not only cold and colorless, but it destroys equalization. Even his falsetto tones, which he seldom used, were supported by sufficient breath, which gave them body and made them sound like mezza voce tones. Here was another important contribution to the remarkable homogeneity of his entire range.

As we have said in an earlier paragraph, Caruso's art consisted of far more than his wonderful instrument; his great industry, which he always applied intelligently, con-

tributed its large share to make him the foremost vocal artist of his time. And to no phase
of his art did he devote more attention than
to the equalization of the voice. One of the
means toward attaining the perfection he
sought and achieved in the equalization of the
voice was long practice of the following exercises in vocalizing. *A* (ah) should be quite
open, with the mouth extended in a horizontal
oval; and the exercise should be sung with
great naturalness and abandon. Gradually,
as Caruso reached the upper range, the open
vowel *A* would insensibly merge into the
vowel *O,* which continued steadily to become
darker in color, or rather to change into the
vowel *U* (oo), precisely as is here graphically
set down:

EXERCISE VI

EXERCISE VI^a

EXERCISE VI^b

EXERCISE VI^c

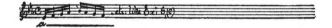

EXERCISE VI^d

EXERCISE VIe

EXERCISE VI^f

EXERCISE VI^g

EXERCISE VI^h

EXERCISE VII

EXERCISE VII^a

Here we must direct the attention of the student to the correct manner of practicing these exercises, reminding him that Caruso said, "with complete abandon of the throat." The gradual blending of the vowels *A, O, U* should therefore take place without any change in the position of the throat during the whole time required for their emission.[1]

[1] See Chapter IX ("Caruso and the Foundation of Vocal Technique") for further details on the pronunciation of the vowels.

Chapter VIII

HOW CARUSO PRACTICED

WHEN I began to work with Caruso, the opulence and splendor of his golden voice, together with the poignancy of his masterly art, had already conquered the vast musical public in the capitals of Europe, as well as the great opera audiences in America. And yet, despite this prodigious achievement, the world-renowned artist worked more industriously than ever, coveting a greater and greater command of his instrument. In fact, there was never a moment during his brilliant career when Caruso complacently sat back and said, "I am satisfied." Animated by the spirit of the sincere artist, intent on his ceaseless effort toward a finer and finer perfection, Caruso had set up standards in vocal art— for himself at least—so rigorous that, however great his progressive attainments, his ideal was always in advance of even his performance. He felt that the genuine artist can never attain to perfection in his own eyes,

141

and that to rest content on what his public may regard as perfection is to die as an artist.

I dwell on this conviction of Enrico Caruso's, on his exacting attitude toward his own art, because it is intimately connected with his manner of practicing and his habits of working. Searching and fearless self-criticism, according to Caruso, is an essential principle which the vocal artist must needs accept; it is the mainspring of uninterrupted progress; it leads the artist to the genuine bel canto. Caruso went much further in his emphasis upon the important principle of effective self-criticism. He said:

"The very talent of an artist is revealed in his ability to detect and understand his shortcomings, and especially in his courage to acknowledge their existence."

No one could have been a severer critic of Caruso's great art than was Caruso himself. He worked with tremendous concentration, and his acute ear was ever to descry the slightest flaw in the tone production, in the quality or the interpretation of a musical passage. It was this infinite care, this minute attention as well to the details as to the larger problems which confront the vocal artist, that in due time made Caruso the complete master of his instrument and of all its manifold resources.

In addition to his great love for his art, Caruso brought a magnificent high-mindedness and a deep sense of responsibility to his profession. "An artist, in order to be worthy of the place he has won for himself in the world of song," Caruso repeatedly remarked to me, "must continually strive for a higher perfection. If he is content with the achievement of the moment, he either recedes, or he is superseded by another artist of more exalted ideals."

But to infer that Caruso derived his artistic ideals from a struggle for place in the field of song would be to insult the memory of a great artist. All who had the good fortune to be his friends know that he deeply loved his art, that he was unsparing in his endeavors to advance it. Not that the spirit of the sportsman was lacking; for it was the sportsman in Caruso that roused his ambition to hold the supreme place among singers, a position for which he battled with such untiring energy. This is a very different matter from the ambition which covets success for its own sake and for its worldly emoluments. That is the win-at-any-cost ambition which we customarily associate with the professional sportsman, the spirit which cultivates pull, which exploits unfair and irrelevant advantages, which is not scrupulous as to the rule of the game, because its gaze is fixed on rewards instead of on excellence. Caruso's ambition, on the other hand, was of the sort we recognize and applaud in the amateur sportsman, whose motto is, "May the best man win," and whose ardent vow is, "By all that I have in me, I mean to be that man." To such a man unearned success must be as bitter as unrewarded excellence.

Accordingly, Caruso was never a victim of the mean temper which degrades opponents in order to enjoy the cheap triumphs of a petty rivalry. It is well known that he was generous in advice and assistance to his fellow-artists. When he was singing with an artist of little vocal power, he would modulate his sonorous voice that he might not overwhelm the less fortunate singer. On one occasion, during a performance of "La Bohème" at the

Metropolitan, Caruso stretched this habitual generosity to an unprecedented degree. The Colline of that night was in poor voice and wished to be replaced by another basso. The management urged and finally persuaded him to see it through in spite of his growing hoarseness. By the time he had reached *Vecchia zimarra senti* the unhappy basso simply could not sing a note. Caruso immediately thrust a cloak over himself and began to sing the famous "Song of the Cloak" with a good bass quality, to the great astonishment of the other singers, the conductor, and those of the audience who recognized the great tenor through his disguise.

Caruso may have counselled some singers to acquire methodical habits; or he may have advised others to retire and rise at regular hours. He may also have suggested that it is more beneficial to practice in the morning, and then, after a rest and some recreation, to do some work in the afternoon. All this advice, all counsel of a similar nature—and Caruso generally offered it whenever it was sought—was sound enough for the singer with an average constitution. In fact, no vocalist can do better than lead a life of moderation, for the fit condition of his vocal organism is entirely dependent upon his physical well-being. What Caruso had steadily in mind was that the singer must not let his manner of living overtax the system whence he draws the motive power for his singing.

Caruso himself, however, had no fixed hours when he retired or arose. It frequently occurred that he got up early the morning following a night on which he had sung; on the other hand, there were times when he got up very late, although he had not sung a note the previous night. He possessed a temperament which was, for some reason or other, averse to rigid regularity. At all events, whether the hours which Caruso reserved for work and sleep were or were not as regular as they should have been, he saw to it that his body received all the necessary rest and exercise.

That Caruso was always full of play is notorious; in fact, it was his almost boyish love of play which prevented a great many people from understanding his real character. It was only natural that many of his pranks, good-natured as their victims knew them to be, should have been misrepresented by the jealous and the envious and have finally reached the public in such colors as made them seem spiteful, so that they added their share to the obstacles which prevented many who admired Caruso the singer from understanding Caruso the man. This is one of the disadvantages of life in the lime-light, a handicap familiar to all whose careers bring them prominently before the public. In Caruso's case its injustice is evidenced by the universal love, almost the idolatry, in which the great singer was held by all who had the good luck to know him personally.

The fact is that Caruso's sense of humor was as wholesome as it was keen. It afforded him a cheerful and unfailing outlet for his overbubbling energy, and that the energy he invested in fun did not merely waste itself through the safety valves of the moment is attested by his remarkable caricatures. Lightly as these were tossed off, they are so effective in their penetration and so trenchant in their wit that they will live long as evidence that singing was not the only art to offer Enrico Caruso a career. In the whole series of his caricatures, however, you will search in vain for anything mean or ill-tempered. They bite but they never snarl; and good nature laughs in every line of them. The hand that dashed them off was no doubt ready enough in practical jokes, but it was incapable of spite.

So active was Caruso, both mentally and physically, that he could remain idle for scarcely an instant of the entire day. He seemed to take an interest in all that went on about him. The pulse of life was indeed in his veins! Although he had no precise hours set aside for his daily vocal work, on days when he was to sing, however, he would rise early and carefully prepare himself, vocally and otherwise, for the occasion.

On rising, Caruso first drank the inevitable cup of coffee, so dear to all Italians. Then he proceeded to spray his throat—as he laughingly said, *pulire lo strumento,* to cleanse the instrument—with a steam atomizer. After thoroughly spraying his throat, he continued with his toilette. While he was thus getting ready for his day's work, I would be at the piano, playing for him the score of the opera he was to sing that night. As he heard the score again, Caruso would hum or whistle the passages with which he was particularly impressed. When he had finally completed his toilette, to which he devoted considerable attention, he felt fresh and vigorous for the rest of the day.

It may not be uninteresting to set down here why Caruso wished me to play the entire score. He was not merely the great tenor, with a marvelous vocal organism; in his own fashion, he was also a great musician. As a consequence, he refused to sacrifice the ensemble of a musical work by disproportionately featuring what he himself was to sing. Caruso possessed a fine sense of measure and proportion, which accounts for his greatness as an ensemble singer. If he desired to shine individually, it was only by dint of his sterling qualities as an artist. He never failed to study the complete score of any opera in which he was to sing; he had to determine for himself at first hand what had been the composer's intention and then thoroughly assimilate the work. This intimate knowledge of the scores stood him in good stead; it helped him considerably in the development of the careful and intelligent plan without which he would sing no rôle; in large measure it aided him to make his interpretations expressive and convincing; it contributed to the authority and, it may almost be said, to the inevitableness of his characterizations.

Caruso frequently commenced the morning's vocal work by practicing vocalises for about ten minutes, and this he usually did whether or not he had a performance that day. During those ten minutes his whole being was intent on his work; his concentration was so great that nothing seemed to escape his acute ear.

Since the absolute control of the breath is the basis of pure bel canto, Caruso would begin with his two exercises for breath control, those reproduced in the chapter on breathing as Exercises I and II (pages 105 and 112). These vocalises he sang in the manner shown in Exercise VI, in the chapter on tone production (page 137), advancing chromatically up to C or C sharp. (The student, however, should not go beyond B flat or B.) For developing the agility of the voice, Caruso also practiced Exercises VII and VII^a, using the same vowels as Exercises VI-VI^h. Caruso sang each exercise in full voice, in a single respiration, and he saw to it that all the air emitted from the lungs was duly transformed into tone.

So much for breath control practice. But breath control, tone production, and vocal equalization are closely related; the achievement of success in one phase of vocal art is dependent upon the successful manipulation of the others. So Caruso used these exercises as well as Exercises IV and V, in the chapter on tone production (page 127), for tonal coloring and quality. The vocalises for volume or intensity, Exercises IV and V, he also practiced in full voice. Caruso sang the sustained G of Exercise IV with much power; it had a penetrating ring; and he held it for a considerable length of time. For this sustained tone work, too, he sometimes practiced Exercise III, which is excellent both for the attainment of accurate pitch and the development of equalization in the vowels.[1]

There was always method and plan in what-

[1] Before appearing on the stage, whether at the opera or at a concert, Caruso usually sang his exercises in the following order: (1) VI, (2) IV, (3) V, (4) II, (5) VII^a.

ever Caruso did; he never worked listlessly,
prompted by the desire to get through with
his routine. He had set before himself an
ideal, and he directed all his powers toward
achieving it. He infused into his exercises
the vital spirit that animated, and made significant, the final product of his labor. Even
when he vocalized, he aimed at much more
than what is normally sought by singers,
namely, flexibility and power. He used the
vocalises with such skill and intelligence that
they prepared his voice for the rôle he was
scheduled to sing that night. Was he to appear in "Rigoletto" or in "La Favorita," in
"L'Elisir d' Amore" or in "La Bohème,"
operas which demand of the tenor dexterity
and grace, Caruso would strive to secure,
through modifying the manner of his practicing, the lyric lightness and flexibility suitable
to those rôles. But if he was scheduled to appear in "Samson et Dalila," in "Pagliacci,"
or in "La Juive," works in which the tenor
rôles are primarily dramatic, Caruso endeavored to make his manner of vocalizing fortify
his voice with the necessary power and dramatic ring which these rôles require.

We do not mean, however, to convey the notion that Caruso was content with the broad classification of his rôles into two groups— lyric and dramatic. He was too subtle a vocal artist to be content with so general a grouping; he went much further in his delineations, not only dramatically but also vocally. So fine were the shadings Caruso drew from his ample vocal resources that he seemed to endow each of the characters he created with a specific and individual quality of voice. For Rodolfo in "La Bohème" he succeeded in finding a tonal coloring that differed in quality from that which he created for the Duke in "Rigoletto." Likewise, in "Samson et Dalila," the vocal expressiveness and nuances that he brought to the rôle of Samson were unlike their parallels for the rôles of Rhadames in "Aïda" or Eléazar in "La Juive." He attuned his voice, in a manner of speech, to the character of the music which he was called upon to sing. In this endeavor Caruso revealed the vital essence, the genuine temper, that makes of the interpreting artist a creator. With such a goal constantly before him while he was practicing what other singers

consider "mere exercises," is it any wonder
that he finally reached the utmost height in
vocal art?

From among the details I have related
about Caruso's procedure in practicing his
vocalises, the young vocal student must take
chief pains to remember the all-important fact
that Caruso practiced them with infinite care
and great mental concentration. His hard
work addressed itself not only to retaining the
vocal mastery which he had achieved, but also
and perhaps even more intensely to perfecting what he had accomplished. So the exercises which Caruso used should commend
themselves excellently to all singers who wish
to improve their breathing power, their tone
production, and the tonal quality of their
vocal mechanism. As regards voices of lower
ranges, these vocalises can easily be made
suitable by lowering the initial notes.

I have said that Caruso usually vocalized
for about ten minutes in the morning, before
he began working on his scores. The young
vocal student must not think, however, that
he is thereby advised to rush through the
vocalises in the brief period of ten minutes.

On the contrary, it is of the utmost importance that the exercises, which Caruso used for the purpose of vocalizing, be practiced with earnest attention and long patience. Special care should be bestowed on the tone attack, which must be clean and clear, never breathy and ragged. When he is vocalizing, the young singer must constantly bear in mind the suggestions offered in the chapters on breathing and tone production. If he cannot do this, it is much better not to practice the exercises at all. For bad singing is ruinous to the voice, whereas silence cannot hurt the vocal organs, and is often, as a matter of fact, beneficial. Whatever the student does, he must never tire his voice by practicing too long at a stretch. The vocal organism is a delicate instrument, and it will not tolerate abuse without showing ill effects.

Before we enter upon the discussion of Caruso's method of practicing his rôles, arias, songs (by old or modern masters), or whatever musical work he happened to be studying or reviewing, we must take into consideration at least two of the traits which were invaluable in his art: his splendid vitality, and the consummate ease with which he sang. For without the possession of these two valuable assets, Caruso could not—and most assuredly would not—have worked so unremittingly. He would have ruined his vocal organism. At times, he could work as long as two hours at a stretch without showing the least signs of fatigue, a phenomenal procedure, indeed, in a vocal artist. But Caruso seemed to be indefatigable, both mentally and physically, and he frequently ceased working only when his rendition of the musical text satisfied him vocally and artistically.

Caruso always sang in full voice, and by full voice is meant the natural power of the vocal organism. However, in order to save his vocal organs, and especially when he was learning a new rôle, or studying any other musical text that was unfamiliar to him, he sometimes whistled or hummed the vocal part while I played the accompaniment.

A great deal has been said about the value of humming as a vocal exercise. It may help certain singers to develop their nasal resonators, the correct use of which is extremely important for tonal coloring. On the other hand, if the tones are made too nasal, they become very disagreeable and worse in effect than the colorless white tones.

Strictly speaking, Caruso never considered humming as a vocal exercise, but rather as a diversion. He used that form of inarticulate vocal production either to familiarize himself with a new musical composition or to rest his voice. When he hummed, he produced a wonderfully colored tone quality of ravishing beauty, a tone resembling the timbre of a fine violoncello. So sonorous and resonant, so round and velvety, were the tones Caruso poured out, that they could not have been surpassed in beauty and opulence by an expert 'cellist playing on an old Italian instrument.

Humming, if correctly practiced, however, will develop the resonance of the voice. The humming of most people sounds like a caterwaul because the jaw, the lips, the tongue, and the vocal membranes are all painfully rigid. Of course, the vocal organs should be in the same position for humming as for good tone production: there should be complete relaxation of the facial muscles, the jaw, and the tongue, just as they are kept when in a state of repose or while sleeping; the lips are to be lightly united. Thus the tone vibrations will neither be deadened by obstructing muscles nor forced through the nose by the strain; instead they will resonate within the nasal cavities and make the notes round and beautiful.

Suppose for a moment that Caruso had been unable to sing without effort or strain. His singing would not only have lacked the richness and purity of delivery which it attained, but he could never have indulged for any length of time in his prolonged manner of study without seriously affecting his voice. There were times when he refused to rest, singing a passage or phrase over and over again, each time with another vocal modulation or coloring, until he got the expression and quality that satisfied his exacting musical taste.

Once Caruso felt that he had grasped the true musical significance of the work he was studying, he invoked all his powers to translate that significance into eloquent expression. In this proceeding, during which there effectively emerged his infinite capacity to take pains, Caruso revealed the fact that within his being vibrated the vital quality of sincerity— the hallmark of the great artist.

CHAPTER IX

CARUSO AND THE FOUNDATION OF VOCAL TECHNIQUE

An interesting story is told of Caffarelli, the wonder singer of the eighteenth century, whose extraordinary voice and masterly art enchanted all who heard him just as Caruso captivated the audiences of our time with his glorious organ and marvelous singing. When Caffarelli presented himself before Porpora, the greatest singing master of his time, the Maestro agreed to teach the gifted young boy provided he would promise to follow all the instructions of his teacher. Young Caffarelli gladly made the promise. Then Porpora gave his pupil a sheet of exercises and kept him at it uninterruptedly. The story runs that whenever Caffarelli complained, the Maestro reminded him of the promise he had made. At the end of five or six years Porpora dismissed his pupil with these words: "Go, my son, I have nothing more to teach you. You are the greatest singer in the world."

Whether this story is false or true, we must, of course, take it with a grain of salt. Porpora sent forth the greatest singers of his time—before Caffarelli he had produced Farinelli—and he must thoroughly have understood the fundamental principles of vocal art. He knew that in order to become a great singer it is necessary to acquire perfect mastery of the vocal organism; which means a complete command of the airblast, of tone production, of pitch, and of the sustained as well as of the florid style of singing. In the vocal music of the eighteenth century the sustained airs required a highly flexible voice, and the fioriture passages and runs an organ of great agility. Porpora was well aware of these facts, for he himself was a prolific composer who wrote, among many other works, at least thirty-six operas which abound with airs of tremendous vocal difficulty.

To his teaching Porpora brought a conception of singing worthy of a great master: art begins where technique ends. This explains the sheet of exercises before which Caffarelli was kept hard at work for a number of years. And when the master said to his pupil, "I have nothing more to teach you," very likely he was speaking from the point of view of vocal technique. According to Porpora, the first aim of the singer should be to overcome all mechanical difficulties, to create a perfect instrument. The vocalist cannot safely make demands upon his instrument when it is imperfect or poorly trained. All the soul and all the interpretative power in the world will be of no avail to the bad singer, for his organ will be incapable of giving artistic expression to his ideas or his emotions.

This fundamental truth about the singer's art Caruso learnt early in his career, and therefore, instead of relying on his naturally beautiful organ, he directed all his efforts toward making it a perfect instrument. Like Porpora, Caruso also believed that art begins only where technique ends, and that the vocal artist must have a thorough technical foundation. Only that can enable him to give adequate expression to his feelings. To be sure, greater demands were made upon the resources of the vocalist in the past than are usually made to-day; and this is especially true of the opera singer. The florid style, with its runs and trills, practically does not appear in modern operas; it is no longer employed as a means of musical expression by the modern composer. Nor do cadenzas or fioriture passages appear often in modern songs. But, aside from the fact that the repertory of the present-day singer must comprise the masterpieces of the past, it is more than ever true that if he wishes to be ranked as a vocal artist of the first magnitude, it is essential that he have the utmost vocal capacity, including the flexibility and agility of the florid singer, in order to be able to render perfectly the dramatic style in the works of modern composers. It is a mistaken notion that the latter require little vocal technique, that a beautiful voice is all that is necessary. As a matter of fact, the intervals and progressions in modern compositions possess difficulties that overtax, and in a brief period ruin, voices which lack the necessary technical foundation.

In setting down in this chapter the exercises with which Caruso used to build up his vocal technique, we are not offering singers a systematic vocal method. If this were our purpose, we should simply be adding one more collection of solfeggi to the numerous collections already in existence. These exercises are principally intended for singers who wish to perfect their technique and for teachers of singing who wish to benefit by the suggestions of the greatest vocal artist of his age and one of the greatest of all time. No singer who practices these exercises must think for a moment that Caruso's vocalises are reproduced here with any intention that they be used as a short cut to attaining perfection. Caruso would have abhorred the idea as downright imposture. There are no short cuts in art. The ease or difficulty with which a singer gradually masters his instrument depends entirely on his aptitude or on the talent which nature has bestowed on him.

It is amazing that singers should think it possible in a very short time to achieve perfection in the difficult art of singing, whereas violinists or pianists take it for granted that they must work for years before they can hope to gain even a partial command of the mechanical difficulties of the violin or the

piano. Is it because singers do not actually
see the mechanism of the vocal organs that
they believe the human voice can be used
effectively without arduous study? There are
no tricks or secrets whereby the vocalist can
magically be turned into a great artist overnight. Caruso was well aware of this truth,
and he impressed it upon the minds of all
who sought his advice. If Caruso preached
anything at all, it was the gospel of work.
Misguided work, or work in the wrong direction, however, will not only be futile, but actually harmful. Singers will do well, therefore,
when they are practicing the exercises which
the great tenor habitually used, to have in
mind Caruso's suggestions on tone production.

For the value which the singer can derive
from these vocalises will be in proportion to
the care with which he practices them. He
must evoke all the concentration at his command, so that he may give the necessary attention to the position of the body and the
head—both should be erect but relaxed—to
the breath control, to the tone attack, and to
the tone production. Nor must he forget to

make sure that every tone be perfect in pitch, for the acquirement of precision in intonation is largely the result of careful practice.

A COLLECTION OF EXERCISES THAT CARUSO USED

EXERCISE I

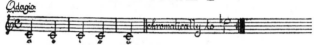

This exercise, which has already been reproduced in the chapter on tone production (Chapter VII), Caruso used for the purpose of fixing the intonation and of securing a steady flow of breath well under his control. Like all the vocalises which he practiced from time to time, according to his needs at the moment, this one may be effectively employed for other purposes than those here indicated; but singers will find it most excellent for the acquirement of precision in pitch and of stability in managing the breath. It is also of value, of course, as a preparation for sustained legato singing. Furthermore, it is admirable as an exercise for the blending of the vowels. Special care and full value must be given to the pronunciation of the vowels, for if their roundness or natural beauty is in any way distorted by unnecessary effort, the muscles of the throat and the mouth get strained, the steady flow of the breath is disturbed, and, as a consequence, the purity of the tone cannot but be destroyed.

Caruso usually practiced this exercise, as well as the others, in full voice, though there were times when he preferred to sing them in mezza voce; it was all a matter of what object he had in view—whether he had to sing, for example, a lyric or a dramatic rôle. When he was scheduled to sing a dramatic rôle, he always vocalized in full voice, and by "full voice" is meant his natural vocal capacity.

EXERCISE II

In practicing this exercise the singer must aim to make the vowels homogeneous throughout the different tones: that is, while he is progressing from one tone to another, the vowel sung should retain the same placement or production and the same intensity. Furthermore, not only must the value of each vowel remain the same throughout the eight tones on which it is sung, but all the five vowels must be alike in placement and in intensity.

EXERCISE III

There can be no beautiful singing without a perfect tone attack. If the tone is not issued with sureness and decision, it will be ragged and breathy, with a tendency to leave the pitch. The above exercise will aid the singer to perfect his tone attack and will afford him practice in the various intervals. This exercise may be sung in all the keys.

EXERCISE IV

EXERCISE V

EXERCISE VI

EXERCISE VII

EXERCISE VIII

EXERCISE IX

EXERCISE X

EXERCISE XI

EXERCISE XII

EXERCISE XIII

EXERCISE XIV

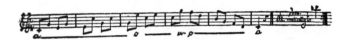

EXERCISE XV

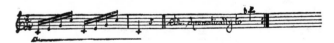

EXERCISE XVI

EXERCISE XVII

EXERCISE XVIII

EXERCISE XIX

EXERCISE XX

EXERCISE XXI

The preceding eighteen vocalises (Exercises IV-XXI) Caruso practiced from time to time in order to maintain at its high level the remarkable agility and suppleness of his voice. He did not always sing the exercises consecutively as they are here set down, but often practiced them as they occurred to him.

As they are reproduced here, the exercises are for tenors and sopranos; but they can eas-

EXERCISE XXII

EXERCISE XXIII

EXERCISE XXIV

ily be modified—and this applies to all the exercises of the book—for voices of lower range.

These three exercises Caruso employed to cultivate flexibility in the jaw, and, although the rapid repetition of *Do* will make both the tongue and the jaw move easily and with agility, the singer must not obstruct the free movement of the two organs by failing to relax them. In this matter, as in all that concerns bel canto, rigidity in any form whatsoever will prevent his attaining the object he has in view—beautiful singing.

EXERCISE XXV

EXERCISE XXVI

EXAMPLES OF PORTAMENTO

Portamento is the carrying of the voice very smoothly from one tone to another. It is a highly effective and expressive embellishment in the art of singing when it is used correctly and with good taste. On the other hand, let the portamento be used poorly and indiscriminately, and it becomes atrocious to the musical ear. In gliding from one tone to the other the singer must beware not to stop at any of the intervening tones; the glide must be smooth and uninterrupted. Nor should the singer employ the portamento too frequently, for it may affect the evenness and clean delivery of his legato singing. Caruso used the portamento with exquisite taste; it infused life and expressiveness into his phrasing. By means of it he often brought out the very character of the music he was singing. Sung with Caruso's mastery, this embellishment becomes one of the most stirring we have in music.

EXERCISE XXVII

Messa di voce (the art of swelling out and diminishing the volume of a sustained tone in one breath) is an ornament of song that was held in high esteem by the great masters of the past; and it is quite worthy of that esteem, for it adds color and eloquence to sustained singing. But if it confers great beauty upon singing, its technique can be mastered only after long practice and diligent work. The singer must attain a notable perfection in the production of simple, sustained tones before he attempts to sing messa di voce; for this device, in order to be effective, requires a highly flexible voice.

There are no secrets for the acquirement of a beautiful messa di voce; it is fundamentally a matter of perfect breath control. (The singer must ever return to his motive power —the breath.) Caruso's messa di voce was marvelous in its effects—as in the last phrase of the flower song in "Carmen," *Carmen, je t'aime*—because he had complete command of his airblast.

Nowadays comparatively few singers are able to deliver a beautiful messa di voce, for the mere reason that they have not acquired

the principles of tone mastery. It is pitiful
to watch a singer with a flushed face, a strained
neck, and a rigid jaw attempting to sing
messa di voce. He imagines that he has only
to exert pressure on his vocal organs, and an
increase in tone will follow. He is soon disillu-
sioned; his tone not only fails to increase, but
is so stifled by the tightened muscles that it
actually decreases in volume. There can be
no beautiful messa di voce unless the vocal
organs are relaxed—the throat and the mouth
should remain as in a state of repose—and the
tone is emitted without strain or effort.

EXERCISE XXVIII

EXERCISE XXIX

These two exercises, which may be sung in
all the keys, the singer will find useful as an
aid toward making the voice both agile and
flexible. Caruso employed them at various

times as preparation for legato, and for legato and staccato, singing. Sometimes also he used them to warm up the voice.

The foregoing collection of exercises throws considerable light on Caruso's comprehensive conception of the technique of the singer's art. He believed in a thorough foundation of vocal technique and was in complete agreement with the views of the great masters of the past. He never entertained the notion that a singer who is the fortunate possessor of an unusual vocal organ can be prepared in six months— or at the utmost in a year—for a life career in opera or on the concert-stage. The insufficiently prepared singers, who have not completely mastered their instruments, let them have never so good voices, enjoy but a brief run of success and disappear as suddenly as they have appeared. They have never really learned how to use their vocal organs, and in their attempts to be emotional and dramatic they bring down upon themselves the inevitable consequence—the ruin of their voices. No vocal artist ever infused more dramatic emotion into song than Caruso; but Caruso's tones, no matter how impassioned or dramatic, were so subject to his vocal mastery that they were never forced or strained and therefore remained mellow and pure. Had not his glorious voice been silenced by a premature death, there is no doubt but that Enrico Caruso would have continued for years to come to pour out his magical music.

In yet another province of the singer's art Caruso was a great master—diction. His purity of diction was in the main the result of the purity with which he emitted his tones. The art of the singer may be likened to an extremely delicate mechanism which may be manipulated effectively if all the component parts are perfect; with one part imperfect, however, the entire mechanism must fail to give satisfactory results. Faulty diction on the part of singers is usually caused by defective tone production. When the vocal organs are forced into rigid contortions, they can by no means be expected to possess eloquence of utterance.

Caruso's vowels were open and pure, full and resonant, because he pronounced them with ease and freedom; and this ease and freedom came from the remarkable suppleness and flexibility of his vocal organs. He had no mysterious secrets; while innumerable less successful singers were seeking far and wide for tricks that would enable them to utter the vowels clearly and musically, Caruso remained loyal to the principles of the great masters of bel canto. Here again, as in the other domains of vocal technique, it was patient study, directed by an alert musical intelligence and an artistic sensitiveness, that finally led Caruso not only to the perfect equalization of the vowels but to the mastery of all the gradations of tonal coloring inherent in them.

Caruso did not set down any hard and fast rules for the correct pronunciation of the vowels, except perhaps those principles to which the vocalist must give heed in order to secure good tone production. The exercises which we have here reproduced for the flexibility of the jaw will aid the singer in pronouncing the vowels with more roundness and eloquence, since the rigidity of the jaw is in great measure responsible for the havoc that is made of their natural beauty. The jaw should remain relaxed so that it will droop loosely; in this position, as in the case of the emission of tones, the jaw will not obstruct the blending or the pure utterance of the vowels.

Nor is there any radical difference in the underlying principle for the clear and distinct enunciation of the consonants; the less effort the singer exerts, the better will be his articulation. In fact, all the evils of the singer are wrought upon him by the employment of unnecessary effort. Caruso's faultless articulation was due to the flexibility of his lips and tongue, and to the fact that he endeavored never to overemphasize the enunciation of the consonants. An excellent exercise for the flexibility of the tongue and lips (and also for the distinct enunciation of the *r*) is: Tra, tre, tri, tro, tru; and Bra, bre, bri, bro, bru (Italian pronounciation).

The singer should remember that the tightening of the articulating organs by undue stress will always tend to distort the clarity and distinctness of his diction. "The articulation of the consonants," said Caruso, "must be effected in the simplest and most natural way, namely, in accordance with the natural movements of the motive organs that are called upon to produce them." This goes to the very bottom of the question. It is the intervention and the obstruction of the unnecessary muscles or organs that destroy the purity of diction as they destroy the purity of tone production.

Caruso always aimed high; it was his ambition to become a master in every domain of vocal technique. All the numerous problems with which the vocalist is confronted are intricately interwoven; indeed, the mastery of one depends on the mastery of another. Caruso reached the highest pinnacles of vocal art because, unlike most singers, he endeavored to become a master in all its provinces.

Chapter X

STYLE AND REPERTORY

WHAT distinguishes art from mechanism is that the one is permeated with individuality whereas the other is the vehicle for impersonal force. Both a work of art and a given mechanical construction may possess perfection in execution; yet the mechanical fabric will leave us cold while the work of art rouses our emotions—moves us. It is further true that the more a work of art is dominated by a strong personality, the greater will be its effect on us. This is just as true of the interpreting artist as of the poet or of the composer. Singing that is not pervaded with personality lacks warmth and magnetism; it fails to stir us. The personal manner, the personal intensity, which the singer reveals in his art conditions his style.

In the vocal art this term *style* is frequently employed most indefinitely. It is by no means unusual to see the expression *style* applied to the singer's method of singing, as if all styles

should not be rendered through the same
vehicle—the method which yields the best
artistic results. Obviously the singer must
aim to interpret whatever he sings—whether
it be the works of seventeenth and eighteenth
century composers or the compositions of
present-day musicians—with the same skill
and expertness, lest he be adjudged incompetent. The breath control and the tone production must needs be managed with the same
mastery when one is singing a recent composition as when he is performing an old masterpiece. Otherwise, from the point of view
of technique, the rendering will be imperfect,
and an imperfect technique means, at the very
best, an immature art. So it is not with the
method of singing that style is concerned.
Nor can it with justice be applied to any external mannerisms of a singer. An affecta-
tion, though paraded with pomp, deceives no
one; if the insincerity does not revolt us, it at
all events leaves us cold.

No, style is that vital quality of sincerity
which comes from the inmost recesses of the
artist's nature. That is what the great
Frenchman meant in his brilliant and pro-

found saying: "The style is the man."
(Buffon hit upon a great truth to which we
must ever return.) Whatever characteristics
the singer's style may disclose, his singing
will be convincing only as it emanates from
his real personality. The greatness of his
style will be in direct ratio to the greatness
of his personality: the one cannot be sepa-
rated from the other. What made Enrico
Caruso a great master of style was the vitali-
zation of whatever he sang by a great personality. He expressed his musical conceptions
and emotions in all their intensity and color,
exactly as he conceived and felt them. It was
this fidelity to his emotions and to his creative
imagination that made his art sincere and bestowed distinction and the sense of inevitableness on all his interpretations.

When Caruso was asked for some light on
the formation and the development of style,
he repeated Talma's illuminating remark:
"The artist must possess a cold head and a
warm heart." In other words, the style of a
singer is created by his mental grasp of the
significance of his emotions. It cannot be acquired in any external manner; it must emerge

from the innermost depths of the singer's being. Otherwise it will remain insignificant
and unconvincing. That is why every attempt
to imitate another's style is ineffective, no
matter how well the imitation may be carried
out. Imitation is the very antithesis of style,
and the musical ear can easily detect the one
from the other. The imitation never fails to
ring false, for it lacks the vital spark with
which a genuine style vitalizes a work of art
to make it quiver with life. But what the
singer must chiefly bear in mind anent the
question of style is that music, more perhaps
than any other art, rests on contrasts and not
on similarities. Accordingly, the style of a
singer is the more distinctive and compelling
as it reveals with greater emphasis the singer's
unique individuality.

So much for the larger aspects of the singer's style, as a manifestation of his intellectual
and emotional constitution. But just as the
style of a composer varies in melody, in harmony, and in rhythm according to the mood
he wishes to express—whether it be joy,
sorrow, passion, religious fervor, or banter—

so the singer must needs vary his style in order to attune it to the character of the music he is to sing. Monteverde, Pergolesi, and Carissimi cannot be sung in the same style as Verdi, Puccini, and Leoncavallo; nor can the latter be interpreted in the same manner as Bizet, Wagner, or Debussy. To be worthy of the name of artist, the singer must so mold his style as to make it appropriate to the composer whom he is interpreting, and, furthermore, he must adopt his style so that it will reveal the character of the particular work he is rendering. His singing must be faithful to his mood, but his mood must reflect the mood of the composer and of the composition.

Caruso was a great interpreter, at his greatest when he was living out upon the stage the life of the character he was representing. And although all that he did bore unmistakably the impress of his own inimitable personality, he could so fashion, shape, and model his own style that each of his diverse interpretations was instinct with individuality. One need only compare his singing of *La donna è mobile* or the *Racconto di Rodolfo* with his singing of Stradella's *Pietà, Signore* or of

Halévy's *Rachel: quand du Seigneur la grâce tutélaire*—to mention only a few of the many superb phonographic records of Caruso's great art—in order to be convinced not only of the larger attributes of Caruso's style, which made his art unique, but of its unusual variety in expression, its flexible representation of his moods as they responded to the significance of the music he was singing. There is grace, lightness, and abandon in his rendering of *La donna è mobile,* and a delicacy of phrasing which enhances its musical value; the sentiment and pathos in the *Racconto di Rodolfo* exhibit a very different aspect of his personality, and the ardor and impassioned eloquence with which he intones Stradella's fervid plea and Halévy's dramatic air demonstrate the wide versatility of his style.

Caruso occupied himself little with considerations of style from an historical point of view. He was always amused when he heard people speak of a seventeenth century or an eighteenth century manner of singing. On such occasions he would laughingly say: "Didn't artists sing with their vocal organs in those good old days?" Yet it must not be thought that he dismissed the whole question quite so superficially as the remark would indicate. Caruso could never resist an opportunity for his wit.

The truth is that he was too great an artist to be hampered by the trammels of crystallized views regarding the interpretation of any musical work, old or modern. "The singer," he would say, "must of course respect the sentiments of the composer. But, after all, the composer is heard through the temperament of the singer, and the singer can only give expression to the ideas and emotions that the musical work arouses in him. Should he endeavor to do otherwise, then the interpretation will lack style and conviction."

Caruso may have taken certain liberties which his extraordinary vocal organism and his powerful pair of bellows permitted, but he was always prompted to these liberties by his desire for finer artistic effects. It was never caprice, for his utmost endeavor went into the effort to vitalize all that he sang with the breath of life, and this gave conviction to all his singing, whether or not he followed servilely the so-called traditional interpretations.

Nothing is so deadly to the art of song as monotony, and monotony is bound to make its appearance in the singer's attempt to efface the emotions which inwardly guide his utterance. What interest, except the historical, can attach to a traditional rendering that is devoid of the personal magnetism of the singer? If he is an artist at all, it is his soul that gives new vitality and life to the musical work he is interpreting, discovering beauties that may have escaped the composer himself. Besides, entirely too much is being said lately of the composer's intentions, which usually prove to vary with the taste of the speaker who propounds them. Whatever the intentions of a composer may have been, his work must not be made insipid and lifeless, devoid of nuance, rhythm, and plan. This should be the prevailing principle in the style of the vocal artist; and it was this ideal that Caruso accepted as his own.

The repertory and the style of Enrico Caruso were closely related: his repertory fashioned and developed his style, and his style widened the scope of his repertory. But both his style and his repertory can be traced to one source—the evolution of his vocal powers. It was this harmony in the different domains of his artistic achievement as a singer that bestowed upon Caruso not only his preëminence but also his uncommon endurance.

Throughout his brilliant career Caruso never attempted to sing a rôle, an aria, or a song that, in his judgment, was beyond his vocal capacity or that was unsuited to his vocal organism. And this in spite of the fact that his was a voice of unusual range and power. Nor did his great dramatic talent affect his decision in the matter of choosing a rôle. He foresaw the inevitable consequences of indulging in parts that lie, vocally speaking, beyond the singer's ability—the untimely ruin of the voice. It was his firm conviction, founded on his thorough understanding of the mechanism of the voice, that the vocal artist can express his ideas and sentiments adequately in song only when he can sing with ease, without laboring over technical difficulties.

For Caruso, his song and his dramatic art

were not merely closely interwoven: they were forged into one entity. Every one of his vocal phrases was developed out of the character represented, out of the situations in which that character participated. And to every character Caruso gave a soul, because Caruso had completely assimilated his nature. As Canio he was a peasant, a rustic, among other peasants; as Cavaradossi he was a child with the soul of a hero; as Eléazar he was a religious visionary inspired by the God of his people. And in every characterization Caruso made his voice play its legitimate part in that perfected unity of portrayal which he had, first of all, established as his ideal.

It is true that he was aided by the fact that his voice was of as captivating softness and rounded fullness in lyric passages (a male voice even in phrases of most delicate pianissimo) as it was full of glow and passion in dramatic moments, when it made his auditors vibrate with emotion. But this rare vocal flexibility was the master's own achievement, too. For his method, based as it was on principles whose application should be universal—his manner of work, the scale and exercise material he used, his manner of breathing, the effortless ease with which he produced his tones, and the remarkable coördination of all the formative elements which made him the great vocal artist—was, when all has been said, one of the products of his genius. The sum of the matter is that Enrico Caruso's vocal mastery brought lustre and conviction to the impersonations of his wide repertory in about the same degree that his dramatic endowment infused the breath of life not only into his many operatic rôles but also into the lyric utterance of his numerous songs by old and modern masters.

The sharp individual coloring, both dramatic and vocal, with which Caruso portrayed all of his impersonations attested both the astonishing breadth of his observation of life and the marvelously versatile skill of his presentation. That his characterizations were as varied as the numerous rôles of his repertory —for no two of them were alike—was due not only to his mastery of singing and his command of declamation, but also to his study of make-up. It is a province of the opera singer's art to which little attention is ordi-

narily given. Indeed, the make-up of most
men and women on the operatic stage is so
banal, so devoid of character, that it is justly
ridiculed by all who seek something more than
beautiful singing at the opera house. What
would a theater audience think of an actor
whose make-up gave him rather the appearance of a puppet than that of the character
he was endeavoring to present? And yet few
opera singers, who are also supposed to look
and act their parts, devote much care to their
make-up.

Caruso was as careful about creating the
appropriate make-up for the character he was
impersonating as he was about studying the
appropriate gestures, declamation, and musical expression. He pondered the mental, emotional, and moral traits of the character as they
were revealed not only in his own lines and
music but throughout the entire opera. If he
found that insufficient, he searched elsewhere
—in art, in literature, in history. When he
was preparing the rôle of Samson, he went
to the Bible for additional enlightenment on
that legendary hero in order that he might
visualize him the more vividly; and, as we have

already remarked, when he was studying
Eléazar, he sought advice on Jewish customs
from a prominent Yiddish actor of New York.
Once Caruso had formed a vivid mental picture of the character he was to enact, the problem of the make-up solved itself.

In the truest sense of the word Caruso was
a *creator* of character. In his effort to make
all his impersonations, down to the minutest
detail, distinctive for their individuality, he
was in some measure helped by his physique.
Caruso was of medium size; and, though the
lines of his face were firmly chiseled, neither
his head nor his features were really very individual in their physiognomy. It was this
fact which enabled him to throw so great a
measure of physical conviction into his many
impersonations. His face was a mobile mask
which naturally adjusted its lines to the character he was interpreting and reflected its
characteristics and peculiarities in the most
colorful manner.

If in his portrayal of folk-types, rôles such
as Canio and Nemorino, he was superb as a
child of nature, at the same time rôles stamped
with the aristocratic hallmark (Edgardo or

the Duke), heroic rôles (Rhadames or Samson), or romantic rôles (Rodolfo or Julien) were no less within the scope of his dramatic talent. In all that he ever did on the stage there lived the feeling for the actual, the real. His rendering of character as well as of song was impermeate with nature, with power and truth. This is sufficiently established by the fact that Caruso's sweeping, compelling effect in human character-delineation is present no less strongly in our recollection than is the enchanting beauty of his song.

Anyone who heard him in the scene of jealousy in the third act of "Carmen," or at the close of the third act of "Aïda," or when he concluded the "Ridi Pagliacci . . .," could scarcely forget those moments, in which a primal outcry seemed to spring from the human soul at a white heat. It was a natural cry, one that came from the soul; and yet it was not the cry of nature. Though offered with the stylized gestures of realism, it was in truth art in its highest manifestations, an art deeply and subtly controlled, with the control never in any way in evidence. No, it was not Caruso's voice alone which made him unique among his colleagues; he was equally preëminent as an actor and as a creator of character. That is what distinguished his magnificent repertory as it did his masterly style.

And now a concluding word on Caruso's gift to the world. His was a life of manifold interests and talents, and in whatever walk of life he chose to exhibit his versatile genius he achieved marked success. The gift that Caruso displayed in caricature was in itself sufficient to make him famous; and had he devoted more time to modeling, he undoubtedly would have attained a distinguished position in the world of sculpture. But he had chosen to devote his life to the art of song, and it is as a great singer that he will be remembered by future generations.

In selecting the art of song for his career he must have been guided by the gods; for, of his manifold talents, it was his supreme genius as a singer that revealed and combined all his greatest qualities. And it is chiefly vocalists and teachers of the vocal art who will not only be inspired by his ideals but will actually benefit from his principles and his great example.

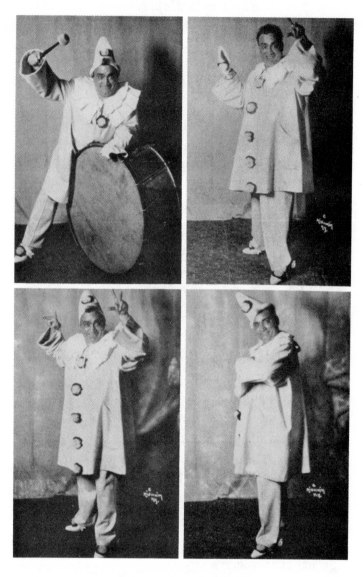

CANIO IN "PAGLIACCI"

RODOLFO IN "LA BOHÈME"

ELÉAZAR IN "LA JUIVE"

A Bas-Relief of Caruso as Eléazar in "La Juive"
Modelled by Himself

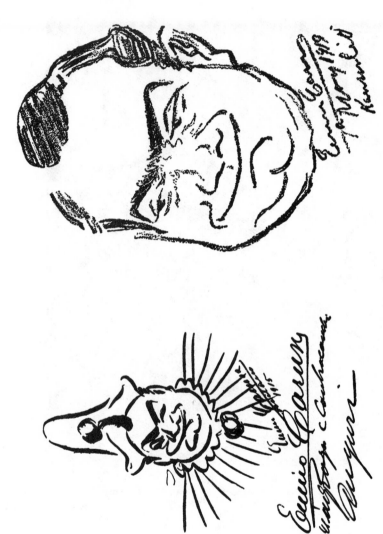

202

SIGNOR FUCITO

SIGNORA FUCITO

AS CARUSO VIEWED HIMSELF

Rhadames in "Aïda"

Don José in "Carmen"

SAMSON IN "SAMSON ET DALILA"

207

DICK JOHNSON IN "THE GIRL OF THE GOLDEN WEST"

CARUSO STUDYING WITH MAESTRO FUCITO

A CATALOG OF SELECTED
DOVER BOOKS
IN ALL FIELDS OF INTEREST

A CATALOG OF SELECTED DOVER
BOOKS IN ALL FIELDS OF INTEREST

CONCERNING THE SPIRITUAL IN ART, Wassily Kandinsky. Pioneering work by father of abstract art. Thoughts on color theory, nature of art. Analysis of earlier masters. 12 illustrations. 80pp. of text. 5⅜ × 8½. 23411-8 Pa. $3.95

ANIMALS: 1,419 Copyright-Free Illustrations of Mammals, Birds, Fish, Insects, etc., Jim Harter (ed.). Clear wood engravings present, in extremely lifelike poses, over 1,000 species of animals. One of the most extensive pictorial sourcebooks of its kind. Captions. Index. 284pp. 9 × 12. 23766-4 Pa. $12.95

CELTIC ART: The Methods of Construction, George Bain. Simple geometric techniques for making Celtic interlacements, spirals, Kells-type initials, animals, humans, etc. Over 500 illustrations. 160pp. 9 × 12. (USO) 22923-8 Pa. $9.95

AN ATLAS OF ANATOMY FOR ARTISTS, Fritz Schider. Most thorough reference work on art anatomy in the world. Hundreds of illustrations, including selections from works by Vesalius, Leonardo, Goya, Ingres, Michelangelo, others. 593 illustrations. 192pp. 7⅛ × 10¼. 20241-0 Pa. $9.95

CELTIC HAND STROKE-BY-STROKE (Irish Half-Uncial from "The Book of Kells"): An Arthur Baker Calligraphy Manual, Arthur Baker. Complete guide to creating each letter of the alphabet in distinctive Celtic manner. Covers hand position, strokes, pens, inks, paper, more. Illustrated. 48pp. 8¼ × 11.
24336-2 Pa. $3.95

EASY ORIGAMI, John Montroll. Charming collection of 32 projects (hat, cup, pelican, piano, swan, many more) specially designed for the novice origami hobbyist. Clearly illustrated easy-to-follow instructions insure that even beginning papercrafters will achieve successful results. 48pp. 8¼ × 11. 27298-2 Pa. $2.95

THE COMPLETE BOOK OF BIRDHOUSE CONSTRUCTION FOR WOOD-WORKERS, Scott D. Campbell. Detailed instructions, illustrations, tables. Also data on bird habitat and instinct patterns. Bibliography. 3 tables. 63 illustrations in 15 figures. 48pp. 5¼ × 8½. 24407-5 Pa. $1.95

BLOOMINGDALE'S ILLUSTRATED 1886 CATALOG: Fashions, Dry Goods and Housewares, Bloomingdale Brothers. Famed merchants' extremely rare catalog depicting about 1,700 products: clothing, housewares, firearms, dry goods, jewelry, more. Invaluable for dating, identifying vintage items. Also, copyright-free graphics for artists, designers. Co-published with Henry Ford Museum & Green-field Village. 160pp. 8¼ × 11. 25780-0 Pa. $9.95

HISTORIC COSTUME IN PICTURES, Braun & Schneider. Over 1,450 costumed figures in clearly detailed engravings—from dawn of civilization to end of 19th century. Captions. Many folk costumes. 256pp. 8⅜ × 11¾. 23150-X Pa. $11.95

STICKLEY CRAFTSMAN FURNITURE CATALOGS, Gustav Stickley and L. & J. G. Stickley. Beautiful, functional furniture in two authentic catalogs from 1910. 594 illustrations, including 277 photos, show settles, rockers, armchairs, reclining chairs, bookcases, desks, tables. 183pp. 6½ × 9¼. 23838-5 Pa. $9.95

AMERICAN LOCOMOTIVES IN HISTORIC PHOTOGRAPHS: 1858 to 1949, Ron Ziel (ed.). A rare collection of 126 meticulously detailed official photographs, called "builder portraits," of American locomotives that majestically chronicle the rise of steam locomotive power in America. Introduction. Detailed captions. xi + 129pp. 9 × 12. 27393-8 Pa. $12.95

AMERICA'S LIGHTHOUSES: An Illustrated History, Francis Ross Holland, Jr. Delightfully written, profusely illustrated fact-filled survey of over 200 American lighthouses since 1716. History, anecdotes, technological advances, more. 240pp. 8 × 10¾. 25576-X Pa. $11.95

TOWARDS A NEW ARCHITECTURE, Le Corbusier. Pioneering manifesto by founder of "International School." Technical and aesthetic theories, views of industry, economics, relation of form to function, "mass-production split" and much more. Profusely illustrated. 320pp. 6⅛ × 9¼. (USO) 25023-7 Pa. $9.95

HOW THE OTHER HALF LIVES, Jacob Riis. Famous journalistic record, exposing poverty and degradation of New York slums around 1900, by major social reformer. 100 striking and influential photographs. 233pp. 10 × 7⅞.
22012-5 Pa $10.95

FRUIT KEY AND TWIG KEY TO TREES AND SHRUBS, William M. Harlow. One of the handiest and most widely used identification aids. Fruit key covers 120 deciduous and evergreen species; twig key 160 deciduous species. Easily used. Over 300 photographs. 126pp. 5⅜ × 8½. 20511-8 Pa. $3.95

COMMON BIRD SONGS, Dr. Donald J. Borror. Songs of 60 most common U.S. birds: robins, sparrows, cardinals, bluejays, finches, more—arranged in order of increasing complexity. Up to 9 variations of songs of each species.
Cassette and manual 99911-4 $8.95

ORCHIDS AS HOUSE PLANTS, Rebecca Tyson Northen. Grow cattleyas and many other kinds of orchids—in a window, in a case, or under artificial light. 63 illustrations. 148pp. 5⅜ × 8½. 23261-1 Pa. $4.95

MONSTER MAZES, Dave Phillips. Masterful mazes at four levels of difficulty. Avoid deadly perils and evil creatures to find magical treasures. Solutions for all 32 exciting illustrated puzzles. 48pp. 8¼ × 11. 26005-4 Pa. $2.95

MOZART'S DON GIOVANNI (DOVER OPERA LIBRETTO SERIES), Wolfgang Amadeus Mozart. Introduced and translated by Ellen H. Bleiler. Standard Italian libretto, with complete English translation. Convenient and thoroughly portable—an ideal companion for reading along with a recording or the performance itself. Introduction. List of characters. Plot summary. 121pp. 5¼ × 8½.
24944-1 Pa. $2.95

TECHNICAL MANUAL AND DICTIONARY OF CLASSICAL BALLET, Gail Grant. Defines, explains, comments on steps, movements, poses and concepts. 15-page pictorial section. Basic book for student, viewer. 127pp. 5⅜ × 8½.
21843-0 Pa. $4.95

BRASS INSTRUMENTS: Their History and Development, Anthony Baines. Authoritative, updated survey of the evolution of trumpets, trombones, bugles, cornets, French horns, tubas and other brass wind instruments. Over 140 illustrations and 48 music examples. Corrected and updated by author. New preface. Bibliography. 320pp. 5⅜ × 8½.   27574-4 Pa. $9.95

HOLLYWOOD GLAMOR PORTRAITS, John Kobal (ed.). 145 photos from 1926–49. Harlow, Gable, Bogart, Bacall; 94 stars in all. Full background on photographers, technical aspects. 160pp. 8⅜ × 11¼.   23352-9 Pa. $11.95

MAX AND MORITZ, Wilhelm Busch. Great humor classic in both German and English. Also 10 other works: "Cat and Mouse," "Plisch and Plumm," etc. 216pp. 5⅜ × 8½.   20181-3 Pa. $5.95

THE RAVEN AND OTHER FAVORITE POEMS, Edgar Allan Poe. Over 40 of the author's most memorable poems: "The Bells," "Ulalume," "Israfel," "To Helen," "The Conqueror Worm," "Eldorado," "Annabel Lee," many more. Alphabetic lists of titles and first lines. 64pp. 5³⁄₁₆ × 8¼.   26685-0 Pa. $1.00

SEVEN SCIENCE FICTION NOVELS, H. G. Wells. The standard collection of the great novels. Complete, unabridged. First Men in the Moon, Island of Dr. Moreau, War of the Worlds, Food of the Gods, Invisible Man, Time Machine, In the Days of the Comet. Total of 1,015pp. 5⅜ × 8½. (USO)   20264-X Clothbd. $29.95

AMULETS AND SUPERSTITIONS, E. A. Wallis Budge. Comprehensive discourse on origin, powers of amulets in many ancient cultures: Arab, Persian, Babylonian, Assyrian, Egyptian, Gnostic, Hebrew, Phoenician, Syriac, etc. Covers cross, swastika, crucifix, seals, rings, stones, etc. 584pp. 5⅜ × 8½. 23573-4 Pa. $12.95

RUSSIAN STORIES/PYCCKNE PACCKA3bl: A Dual-Language Book, edited by Gleb Struve. Twelve tales by such masters as Chekhov, Tolstoy, Dostoevsky, Pushkin, others. Excellent word-for-word English translations on facing pages, plus teaching and study aids, Russian/English vocabulary, biographical/critical introductions, more. 416pp. 5⅜ × 8½.   26244-8 Pa. $8.95

PHILADELPHIA THEN AND NOW: 60 Sites Photographed in the Past and Present, Kenneth Finkel and Susan Oyama. Rare photographs of City Hall, Logan Square, Independence Hall, Betsy Ross House, other landmarks juxtaposed with contemporary views. Captures changing face of historic city. Introduction. Captions. 128pp. 8¼ × 11.   25790-8 Pa. $9.95

AIA ARCHITECTURAL GUIDE TO NASSAU AND SUFFOLK COUNTIES, LONG ISLAND, The American Institute of Architects, Long Island Chapter, and the Society for the Preservation of Long Island Antiquities. Comprehensive, well-researched and generously illustrated volume brings to life over three centuries of Long Island's great architectural heritage. More than 240 photographs with authoritative, extensively detailed captions. 176pp. 8¼ × 11.   26946-9 Pa. $14.95

NORTH AMERICAN INDIAN LIFE: Customs and Traditions of 23 Tribes, Elsie Clews Parsons (ed.). 27 fictionalized essays by noted anthropologists examine religion, customs, government, additional facets of life among the Winnebago, Crow, Zuni, Eskimo, other tribes. 480pp. 6⅛ × 9¼.   27377-6 Pa. $10.95

FRANK LLOYD WRIGHT'S HOLLYHOCK HOUSE, Donald Hoffmann. Lavishly illustrated, carefully documented study of one of Wright's most controversial residential designs. Over 120 photographs, floor plans, elevations, etc. Detailed perceptive text by noted Wright scholar. Index. 128pp. 9¼ × 10¾.
27133-1 Pa. $11.95

THE MALE AND FEMALE FIGURE IN MOTION: 60 Classic Photographic Sequences, Eadweard Muybridge. 60 true-action photographs of men and women walking, running, climbing, bending, turning, etc., reproduced from rare 19th-century masterpiece. vi + 121pp. 9 × 12.
24745-7 Pa. $10.95

1001 QUESTIONS ANSWERED ABOUT THE SEASHORE, N. J. Berrill and Jacquelyn Berrill. Queries answered about dolphins, sea snails, sponges, starfish, fishes, shore birds, many others. Covers appearance, breeding, growth, feeding, much more. 305pp. 5¼ × 8¼.
23366-9 Pa. $7.95

GUIDE TO OWL WATCHING IN NORTH AMERICA, Donald S. Heintzelman. Superb guide offers complete data and descriptions of 19 species: barn owl, screech owl, snowy owl, many more. Expert coverage of owl-watching equipment, conservation, migrations and invasions, etc. Guide to observing sites. 84 illustrations. xiii + 193pp. 5⅜ × 8½.
27344-X Pa. $8.95

MEDICINAL AND OTHER USES OF NORTH AMERICAN PLANTS: A Historical Survey with Special Reference to the Eastern Indian Tribes, Charlotte Erichsen-Brown. Chronological historical citations document 500 years of usage of plants, trees, shrubs native to eastern Canada, northeastern U.S. Also complete identifying information. 343 illustrations. 544pp. 6½ × 9¼.
25951-X Pa. $12.95

STORYBOOK MAZES, Dave Phillips. 23 stories and mazes on two-page spreads: Wizard of Oz, Treasure Island, Robin Hood, etc. Solutions. 64pp. 8¼ × 11.
23628-5 Pa. $2.95

NEGRO FOLK MUSIC, U.S.A., Harold Courlander. Noted folklorist's scholarly yet readable analysis of rich and varied musical tradition. Includes authentic versions of over 40 folk songs. Valuable bibliography and discography. xi + 324pp. 5⅜ × 8½.
27350-4 Pa. $7.95

MOVIE-STAR PORTRAITS OF THE FORTIES, John Kobal (ed.). 163 glamor, studio photos of 106 stars of the 1940s: Rita Hayworth, Ava Gardner, Marlon Brando, Clark Gable, many more. 176pp. 8⅜ × 11¼.
23546-7 Pa. $11.95

BENCHLEY LOST AND FOUND, Robert Benchley. Finest humor from early 30s, about pet peeves, child psychologists, post office and others. Mostly unavailable elsewhere. 73 illustrations by Peter Arno and others. 183pp. 5⅜ × 8½.
22410-4 Pa. $5.95

YEKL and THE IMPORTED BRIDEGROOM AND OTHER STORIES OF YIDDISH NEW YORK, Abraham Cahan. Film Hester Street based on Yekl (1896). Novel, other stories among first about Jewish immigrants on N.Y.'s East Side. 240pp. 5⅜ × 8½.
22427-9 Pa. $6.95

SELECTED POEMS, Walt Whitman. Generous sampling from *Leaves of Grass*. Twenty-four poems include "I Hear America Singing," "Song of the Open Road," "I Sing the Body Electric," "When Lilacs Last in the Dooryard Bloom'd," "O Captain! My Captain!"—all reprinted from an authoritative edition. Lists of titles and first lines. 128pp. 5³⁄₁₆ × 8¼.
26878-0 Pa. $1.00

THE BEST TALES OF HOFFMANN, E. T. A. Hoffmann. 10 of Hoffmann's most important stories: "Nutcracker and the King of Mice," "The Golden Flowerpot," etc. 458pp. 5⅜ × 8½. 21793-0 Pa. $8.95

FROM FETISH TO GOD IN ANCIENT EGYPT, E. A. Wallis Budge. Rich detailed survey of Egyptian conception of "God" and gods, magic, cult of animals, Osiris, more. Also, superb English translations of hymns and legends. 240 illustrations. 545pp. 5⅜ × 8½. 25803-3 Pa. $11.95

FRENCH STORIES/CONTES FRANÇAIS: A Dual-Language Book, Wallace Fowlie. Ten stories by French masters, Voltaire to Camus: "Micromegas" by Voltaire; "The Atheist's Mass" by Balzac; "Minuet" by de Maupassant; "The Guest" by Camus, six more. Excellent English translations on facing pages. Also French-English vocabulary list, exercises, more. 352pp. 5⅜ × 8½. 26443-2 Pa. $8.95

CHICAGO AT THE TURN OF THE CENTURY IN PHOTOGRAPHS: 122 Historic Views from the Collections of the Chicago Historical Society, Larry A. Viskochil. Rare large-format prints offer detailed views of City Hall, State Street, the Loop, Hull House, Union Station, many other landmarks, circa 1904–1913. Introduction. Captions. Maps. 144pp. 9⅜ × 12¼. 24656-6 Pa. $12.95

OLD BROOKLYN IN EARLY PHOTOGRAPHS, 1865–1929, William Lee Younger. Luna Park, Gravesend race track, construction of Grand Army Plaza, moving of Hotel Brighton, etc. 157 previously unpublished photographs. 165pp. 8⅞ × 11¾. 23587-4 Pa. $13.95

THE MYTHS OF THE NORTH AMERICAN INDIANS, Lewis Spence. Rich anthology of the myths and legends of the Algonquins, Iroquois, Pawnees and Sioux, prefaced by an extensive historical and ethnological commentary. 36 illustrations. 480pp. 5⅜ × 8½. 25967-6 Pa. $8.95

AN ENCYCLOPEDIA OF BATTLES: Accounts of Over 1,560 Battles from 1479 B.C. to the Present, David Eggenberger. Essential details of every major battle in recorded history from the first battle of Megiddo in 1479 B.C. to Grenada in 1984. List of Battle Maps. New Appendix covering the years 1967–1984. Index. 99 illustrations. 544pp. 6½ × 9¼. 24913-1 Pa. $14.95

SAILING ALONE AROUND THE WORLD, Captain Joshua Slocum. First man to sail around the world, alone, in small boat. One of great feats of seamanship told in delightful manner. 67 illustrations. 294pp. 5⅜ × 8½. 20326-3 Pa. $5.95

ANARCHISM AND OTHER ESSAYS, Emma Goldman. Powerful, penetrating, prophetic essays on direct action, role of minorities, prison reform, puritan hypocrisy, violence, etc. 271pp. 5⅜ × 8½. 22484-8 Pa. $5.95

MYTHS OF THE HINDUS AND BUDDHISTS, Ananda K. Coomaraswamy and Sister Nivedita. Great stories of the epics; deeds of Krishna, Shiva, taken from puranas, Vedas, folk tales; etc. 32 illustrations. 400pp. 5⅜ × 8½. 21759-0 Pa. $9.95

BEYOND PSYCHOLOGY, Otto Rank. Fear of death, desire of immortality, nature of sexuality, social organization, creativity, according to Rankian system. 291pp. 5⅜ × 8½. 20485-5 Pa. $8.95

A THEOLOGICO-POLITICAL TREATISE, Benedict Spinoza. Also contains unfinished Political Treatise. Great classic on religious liberty, theory of government on common consent. R. Elwes translation. Total of 421pp. 5⅜ × 8½. 20249-6 Pa. $8.95

MY BONDAGE AND MY FREEDOM, Frederick Douglass. Born a slave, Douglass became outspoken force in antislavery movement. The best of Douglass' autobiographies. Graphic description of slave life. 464pp. 5⅜ × 8½. 22457-0 Pa. $8.95

FOLLOWING THE EQUATOR: A Journey Around the World, Mark Twain. Fascinating humorous account of 1897 voyage to Hawaii, Australia, India, New Zealand, etc. Ironic, bemused reports on peoples, customs, climate, flora and fauna, politics, much more. 197 illustrations. 720pp. 5⅜ × 8½. 26113-1 Pa. $15.95

THE PEOPLE CALLED SHAKERS, Edward D. Andrews. Definitive study of Shakers: origins, beliefs, practices, dances, social organization, furniture and crafts, etc. 33 illustrations. 351pp. 5⅜ × 8½. 21081-2 Pa. $8.95

THE MYTHS OF GREECE AND ROME, H. A. Guerber. A classic of mythology, generously illustrated, long prized for its simple, graphic, accurate retelling of the principal myths of Greece and Rome, and for its commentary on their origins and significance. With 64 illustrations by Michelangelo, Raphael, Titian, Rubens, Canova, Bernini and others. 480pp. 5⅜ × 8½. 27584-1 Pa. $9.95

PSYCHOLOGY OF MUSIC, Carl E. Seashore. Classic work discusses music as a medium from psychological viewpoint. Clear treatment of physical acoustics, auditory apparatus, sound perception, development of musical skills, nature of musical feeling, host of other topics. 88 figures. 408pp. 5⅜ × 8½. 21851-1 Pa. $9.95

THE PHILOSOPHY OF HISTORY, Georg W. Hegel. Great classic of Western thought develops concept that history is not chance but rational process, the evolution of freedom. 457pp. 5⅜ × 8½. 20112-0 Pa. $9.95

THE BOOK OF TEA, Kakuzo Okakura. Minor classic of the Orient: entertaining, charming explanation, interpretation of traditional Japanese culture in terms of tea ceremony. 94pp. 5⅜ × 8½. 20070-1 Pa. $3.95

LIFE IN ANCIENT EGYPT, Adolf Erman. Fullest, most thorough, detailed older account with much not in more recent books, domestic life, religion, magic, medicine, commerce, much more. Many illustrations reproduce tomb paintings, carvings, hieroglyphs, etc. 597pp. 5⅜ × 8½. 22632-8 Pa. $10.95

SUNDIALS, Their Theory and Construction, Albert Waugh. Far and away the best, most thorough coverage of ideas, mathematics concerned, types, construction, adjusting anywhere. Simple, nontechnical treatment allows even children to build several of these dials. Over 100 illustrations. 230pp. 5⅜ × 8½. 22947-5 Pa. $7.95

DYNAMICS OF FLUIDS IN POROUS MEDIA, Jacob Bear. For advanced students of ground water hydrology, soil mechanics and physics, drainage and irrigation engineering, and more. 335 illustrations. Exercises, with answers. 784pp. 6⅛ × 9¼. 65675-6 Pa. $19.95

SONGS OF EXPERIENCE: Facsimile Reproduction with 26 Plates in Full Color, William Blake. 26 full-color plates from a rare 1826 edition. Includes "The Tyger," "London," "Holy Thursday," and other poems. Printed text of poems. 48pp. 5¼ × 7. 24636-1 Pa. $4.95

OLD-TIME VIGNETTES IN FULL COLOR, Carol Belanger Grafton (ed.). Over 390 charming, often sentimental illustrations, selected from archives of Victorian graphics—pretty women posing, children playing, food, flowers, kittens and puppies, smiling cherubs, birds and butterflies, much more. All copyright-free. 48pp. 9¼ × 12¼. 27269-9 Pa. $5.95

PERSPECTIVE FOR ARTISTS, Rex Vicat Cole. Depth, perspective of sky and sea, shadows, much more, not usually covered. 391 diagrams, 81 reproductions of drawings and paintings. 279pp. 5⅜ × 8½. 22487-2 Pa. $6.95

DRAWING THE LIVING FIGURE, Joseph Sheppard. Innovative approach to artistic anatomy focuses on specifics of surface anatomy, rather than muscles and bones. Over 170 drawings of live models in front, back and side views, and in widely varying poses. Accompanying diagrams. 177 illustrations. Introduction. Index. 144pp. 8⅜ × 11¼. 26723-7 Pa. $8.95

GOTHIC AND OLD ENGLISH ALPHABETS: 100 Complete Fonts, Dan X. Solo. Add power, elegance to posters, signs, other graphics with 100 stunning copyright-free alphabets: Blackstone, Dolbey, Germania, 97 more—including many lower-case, numerals, punctuation marks. 104pp. 8⅛ × 11. 24695-7 Pa. $8.95

HOW TO DO BEADWORK, Mary White. Fundamental book on craft from simple projects to five-bead chains and woven works. 106 illustrations. 142pp. 5⅜ × 8. 20697-1 Pa. $4.95

THE BOOK OF WOOD CARVING, Charles Marshall Sayers. Finest book for beginners discusses fundamentals and offers 34 designs. "Absolutely first rate . . . well thought out and well executed."—E. J. Tangerman. 118pp. 7¾ × 10⅝. 23654-4 Pa. $5.95

ILLUSTRATED CATALOG OF CIVIL WAR MILITARY GOODS: Union Army Weapons, Insignia, Uniform Accessories, and Other Equipment, Schuyler, Hartley, and Graham. Rare, profusely illustrated 1846 catalog includes Union Army uniform and dress regulations, arms and ammunition, coats, insignia, flags, swords, rifles, etc. 226 illustrations. 160pp. 9 × 12. 24939-5 Pa. $10.95

WOMEN'S FASHIONS OF THE EARLY 1900s: An Unabridged Republication of "New York Fashions, 1909," National Cloak & Suit Co. Rare catalog of mail-order fashions documents women's and children's clothing styles shortly after the turn of the century. Captions offer full descriptions, prices. Invaluable resource for fashion, costume historians. Approximately 725 illustrations. 128pp. 8⅜ × 11¼. 27276-1 Pa. $11.95

THE 1912 AND 1915 GUSTAV STICKLEY FURNITURE CATALOGS, Gustav Stickley. With over 200 detailed illustrations and descriptions, these two catalogs are essential reading and reference materials and identification guides for Stickley furniture. Captions cite materials, dimensions and prices. 112pp. 6½ × 9¼. 26676-1 Pa. $9.95

EARLY AMERICAN LOCOMOTIVES, John H. White, Jr. Finest locomotive engravings from early 19th century: historical (1804–74), main-line (after 1870), special, foreign, etc. 147 plates. 142pp. 11⅜ × 8¼. 22772-3 Pa. $10.95

THE TALL SHIPS OF TODAY IN PHOTOGRAPHS, Frank O. Braynard. Lavishly illustrated tribute to nearly 100 majestic contemporary sailing vessels: Amerigo Vespucci, Clearwater, Constitution, Eagle, Mayflower, Sea Cloud, Victory, many more. Authoritative captions provide statistics, background on each ship. 190 black-and-white photographs and illustrations. Introduction. 128pp. 8⅞ × 11¾. 27163-3 Pa. $13.95

EARLY NINETEENTH-CENTURY CRAFTS AND TRADES, Peter Stockham (ed.). Extremely rare 1807 volume describes to youngsters the crafts and trades of the day: brickmaker, weaver, dressmaker, bookbinder, ropemaker, saddler, many more. Quaint prose, charming illustrations for each craft. 20 black-and-white line illustrations. 192pp. 4⅝ × 6. 27293-1 Pa. $4.95

VICTORIAN FASHIONS AND COSTUMES FROM HARPER'S BAZAR, 1867–1898, Stella Blum (ed.). Day costumes, evening wear, sports clothes, shoes, hats, other accessories in over 1,000 detailed engravings. 320pp. 9⅜ × 12¼.
22990-4 Pa. $13.95

GUSTAV STICKLEY, THE CRAFTSMAN, Mary Ann Smith. Superb study surveys broad scope of Stickley's achievement, especially in architecture. Design philosophy, rise and fall of the Craftsman empire, descriptions and floor plans for many Craftsman houses, more. 86 black-and-white halftones. 31 line illustrations. Introduction. 208pp. 6½ × 9¼. 27210-9 Pa. $9.95

THE LONG ISLAND RAIL ROAD IN EARLY PHOTOGRAPHS, Ron Ziel. Over 220 rare photos, informative text document origin (1844) and development of rail service on Long Island. Vintage views of early trains, locomotives, stations, passengers, crews, much more. Captions. 8⅞ × 11¾. 26301-0 Pa. $13.95

THE BOOK OF OLD SHIPS: From Egyptian Galleys to Clipper Ships, Henry B. Culver. Superb, authoritative history of sailing vessels, with 80 magnificent line illustrations. Galley, bark, caravel, longship, whaler, many more. Detailed, informative text on each vessel by noted naval historian. Introduction. 256pp. 5⅜ × 8½. 27332-6 Pa. $6.95

TEN BOOKS ON ARCHITECTURE, Vitruvius. The most important book ever written on architecture. Early Roman aesthetics, technology, classical orders, site selection, all other aspects. Morgan translation. 331pp. 5⅜ × 8½. 20645-9 Pa. $8.95

THE HUMAN FIGURE IN MOTION, Eadweard Muybridge. More than 4,500 stopped-action photos, in action series, showing undraped men, women, children jumping, lying down, throwing, sitting, wrestling, carrying, etc. 390pp. 7⅞ × 10⅝. 20204-6 Clothbd. $24.95

TREES OF THE EASTERN AND CENTRAL UNITED STATES AND CANADA, William M. Harlow. Best one-volume guide to 140 trees. Full descriptions, woodlore, range, etc. Over 600 illustrations. Handy size. 288pp. 4½ × 6⅜.
20395-6 Pa. $5.95

SONGS OF WESTERN BIRDS, Dr. Donald J. Borror. Complete song and call repertoire of 60 western species, including flycatchers, juncoes, cactus wrens, many more—includes fully illustrated booklet.   Cassette and manual 99913-0 $8.95

GROWING AND USING HERBS AND SPICES, Milo Miloradovich. Versatile handbook provides all the information needed for cultivation and use of all the herbs and spices available in North America. 4 illustrations. Index. Glossary. 236pp. 5⅜ × 8½. 25058-X Pa. $6.95

BIG BOOK OF MAZES AND LABYRINTHS, Walter Shepherd. 50 mazes and labyrinths in all—classical, solid, ripple, and more—in one great volume. Perfect inexpensive puzzler for clever youngsters. Full solutions. 112pp. 8⅛ × 11.
22951-3 Pa. $4.95

PIANO TUNING, J. Cree Fischer. Clearest, best book for beginner, amateur. Simple repairs, raising dropped notes, tuning by easy method of flattened fifths. No previous skills needed. 4 illustrations. 201pp. 5⅜ × 8½. 23267-0 Pa. $5.95

A SOURCE BOOK IN THEATRICAL HISTORY, A. M. Nagler. Contemporary observers on acting, directing, make-up, costuming, stage props, machinery, scene design, from Ancient Greece to Chekhov. 611pp. 5⅜ × 8½. 20515-0 Pa. $11.95

THE COMPLETE NONSENSE OF EDWARD LEAR, Edward Lear. All nonsense limericks, zany alphabets, Owl and Pussycat, songs, nonsense botany, etc., illustrated by Lear. Total of 320pp. 5⅜ × 8½. (USO) 20167-8 Pa. $6.95

VICTORIAN PARLOUR POETRY: An Annotated Anthology, Michael R. Turner. 117 gems by Longfellow, Tennyson, Browning, many lesser-known poets. "The Village Blacksmith," "Curfew Must Not Ring Tonight," "Only a Baby Small," dozens more, often difficult to find elsewhere. Index of poets, titles, first lines. xxiii + 325pp. 5⅜ × 8¼. 27044-0 Pa. $8.95

DUBLINERS, James Joyce. Fifteen stories offer vivid, tightly focused observations of the lives of Dublin's poorer classes. At least one, "The Dead," is considered a masterpiece. Reprinted complete and unabridged from standard edition. 160pp. 5 3/16 × 8¼. 26870-5 Pa. $1.00

THE HAUNTED MONASTERY and THE CHINESE MAZE MURDERS, Robert van Gulik. Two full novels by van Gulik, set in 7th-century China, continue adventures of Judge Dee and his companions. An evil Taoist monastery, seemingly supernatural events; overgrown topiary maze hides strange crimes. 27 illustrations. 328pp. 5⅜ × 8½. 23502-5 Pa. $7.95

THE BOOK OF THE SACRED MAGIC OF ABRAMELIN THE MAGE, translated by S. MacGregor Mathers. Medieval manuscript of ceremonial magic. Basic document in Aleister Crowley, Golden Dawn groups. 268pp. 5⅜ × 8½. 23211-5 Pa. $8.95

NEW RUSSIAN-ENGLISH AND ENGLISH-RUSSIAN DICTIONARY, M. A. O'Brien. This is a remarkably handy Russian dictionary, containing a surprising amount of information, including over 70,000 entries. 366pp. 4½ × 6⅛. 20208-9 Pa. $9.95

HISTORIC HOMES OF THE AMERICAN PRESIDENTS, Second, Revised Edition, Irvin Haas. A traveler's guide to American Presidential homes, most open to the public, depicting and describing homes occupied by every American President from George Washington to George Bush. With visiting hours, admission charges, travel routes. 175 photographs. Index. 160pp. 8¼ × 11. 26751-2 Pa. $10.95

NEW YORK IN THE FORTIES, Andreas Feininger. 162 brilliant photographs by the well-known photographer, formerly with *Life* magazine. Commuters, shoppers, Times Square at night, much else from city at its peak. Captions by John von Hartz. 181pp. 9¼ × 10¾. 23585-8 Pa. $12.95

INDIAN SIGN LANGUAGE, William Tomkins. Over 525 signs developed by Sioux and other tribes. Written instructions and diagrams. Also 290 pictographs. 111pp. 6⅛ × 9¼. 22029-X Pa. $3.50

ANATOMY: A Complete Guide for Artists, Joseph Sheppard. A master of figure drawing shows artists how to render human anatomy convincingly. Over 460 illustrations. 224pp. 8⅜ × 11¼. 27279-6 Pa. $10.95

MEDIEVAL CALLIGRAPHY: Its History and Technique, Marc Drogin. Spirited history, comprehensive instruction manual covers 13 styles (ca. 4th century thru 15th). Excellent photographs; directions for duplicating medieval techniques with modern tools. 224pp. 8⅜ × 11¼. 26142-5 Pa. $11.95

DRIED FLOWERS: How to Prepare Them, Sarah Whitlock and Martha Rankin. Complete instructions on how to use silica gel, meal and borax, perlite aggregate, sand and borax, glycerine and water to create attractive permanent flower arrangements. 12 illustrations. 32pp. 5⅜ × 8½. 21802-3 Pa. $1.00

EASY-TO-MAKE BIRD FEEDERS FOR WOODWORKERS, Scott D. Campbell. Detailed, simple-to-use guide for designing, constructing, caring for and using feeders. Text, illustrations for 12 classic and contemporary designs. 96pp. 5⅜ × 8½. 25847-5 Pa. $2.95

OLD-TIME CRAFTS AND TRADES, Peter Stockham. An 1807 book created to teach children about crafts and trades open to them as future careers. It describes in detailed, nontechnical terms 24 different occupations, among them coachmaker, gardener, hairdresser, lacemaker, shoemaker, wheelwright, copper-plate printer, milliner, trunkmaker, merchant and brewer. Finely detailed engravings illustrate each occupation. 192pp. 4⅝ × 6. 27398-9 Pa. $4.95

THE HISTORY OF UNDERCLOTHES, C. Willett Cunnington and Phyllis Cunnington. Fascinating, well-documented survey covering six centuries of English undergarments, enhanced with over 100 illustrations: 12th-century laced-up bodice, footed long drawers (1795), 19th-century bustles, 19th-century corsets for men, Victorian "bust improvers," much more. 272pp. 5⅜ × 8¼. 27124-2 Pa. $9.95

ARTS AND CRAFTS FURNITURE: The Complete Brooks Catalog of 1912, Brooks Manufacturing Co. Photos and detailed descriptions of more than 150 now very collectible furniture designs from the Arts and Crafts movement depict davenports, settees, buffets, desks, tables, chairs, bedsteads, dressers and more, all built of solid, quarter-sawed oak. Invaluable for students and enthusiasts of antiques, Americana and the decorative arts. 80pp. 6½ × 9¼. 27471-3 Pa. $7.95

HOW WE INVENTED THE AIRPLANE: An Illustrated History, Orville Wright. Fascinating firsthand account covers early experiments, construction of planes and motors, first flights, much more. Introduction and commentary by Fred C. Kelly. 76 photographs. 96pp. 8¼ × 11. 25662-6 Pa. $8.95

THE ARTS OF THE SAILOR: Knotting, Splicing and Ropework, Hervey Garrett Smith. Indispensable shipboard reference covers tools, basic knots and useful hitches; handsewing and canvas work, more. Over 100 illustrations. Delightful reading for sea lovers. 256pp. 5⅜ × 8½. 26440-8 Pa. $7.95

FRANK LLOYD WRIGHT'S FALLINGWATER: The House and Its History, Second, Revised Edition, Donald Hoffmann. A total revision—both in text and illustrations—of the standard document on Fallingwater, the boldest, most personal architectural statement of Wright's mature years, updated with valuable new material from the recently opened Frank Lloyd Wright Archives. "Fascinating"—*The New York Times*. 116 illustrations. 128pp. 9¼ × 10¾. 27430-6 Pa. $10.95

PHOTOGRAPHIC SKETCHBOOK OF THE CIVIL WAR, Alexander Gardner. 100 photos taken on field during the Civil War. Famous shots of Manassas, Harper's Ferry, Lincoln, Richmond, slave pens, etc. 244pp. 10⅝ × 8¼.
22731-6 Pa. $9.95

FIVE ACRES AND INDEPENDENCE, Maurice G. Kains. Great back-to-the-land classic explains basics of self-sufficient farming. The one book to get. 95 illustrations. 397pp. 5⅜ × 8½.
20974-1 Pa. $7.95

SONGS OF EASTERN BIRDS, Dr. Donald J. Borror. Songs and calls of 60 species most common to eastern U.S.: warblers, woodpeckers, flycatchers, thrushes, larks, many more in high-quality recording.
Cassette and manual 99912-2 $8.95

A MODERN HERBAL, Margaret Grieve. Much the fullest, most exact, most useful compilation of herbal material. Gigantic alphabetical encyclopedia, from aconite to zedoary, gives botanical information, medical properties, folklore, economic uses, much else. Indispensable to serious reader. 161 illustrations. 888pp. 6½ × 9¼. 2-vol. set. (USO)
Vol. I: 22798-7 Pa. $9.95
Vol. II: 22799-5 Pa. $9.95

HIDDEN TREASURE MAZE BOOK, Dave Phillips. Solve 34 challenging mazes accompanied by heroic tales of adventure. Evil dragons, people-eating plants, bloodthirsty giants, many more dangerous adversaries lurk at every twist and turn. 34 mazes, stories, solutions. 48pp. 8¼ × 11.
24566-7 Pa. $2.95

LETTERS OF W. A. MOZART, Wolfgang A. Mozart. Remarkable letters show bawdy wit, humor, imagination, musical insights, contemporary musical world; includes some letters from Leopold Mozart. 276pp. 5⅜ × 8½.
22859-2 Pa. $7.95

BASIC PRINCIPLES OF CLASSICAL BALLET, Agrippina Vaganova. Great Russian theoretician, teacher explains methods for teaching classical ballet. 118 illustrations. 175pp. 5⅜ × 8½.
22036-2 Pa. $4.95

THE JUMPING FROG, Mark Twain. Revenge edition. The original story of The Celebrated Jumping Frog of Calaveras County, a hapless French translation, and Twain's hilarious "retranslation" from the French. 12 illustrations. 66pp. 5⅜ × 8½.
22686-7 Pa. $3.95

BEST REMEMBERED POEMS, Martin Gardner (ed.). The 126 poems in this superb collection of 19th- and 20th-century British and American verse range from Shelley's "To a Skylark" to the impassioned "Renascence" of Edna St. Vincent Millay and to Edward Lear's whimsical "The Owl and the Pussycat." 224pp. 5⅜ × 8½.
27165-X Pa. $4.95

COMPLETE SONNETS, William Shakespeare. Over 150 exquisite poems deal with love, friendship, the tyranny of time, beauty's evanescence, death and other themes in language of remarkable power, precision and beauty. Glossary of archaic terms. 80pp. 5³⁄₁₆ × 8¼.
26686-9 Pa. $1.00

BODIES IN A BOOKSHOP, R. T. Campbell. Challenging mystery of blackmail and murder with ingenious plot and superbly drawn characters. In the best tradition of British suspense fiction. 192pp. 5⅜ × 8½.
24720-1 Pa. $5.95

THE WIT AND HUMOR OF OSCAR WILDE, Alvin Redman (ed.). More than 1,000 ripostes, paradoxes, wisecracks: Work is the curse of the drinking classes; I can resist everything except temptation; etc. 258pp. 5⅜ × 8½. 20602-5 Pa. $5.95

SHAKESPEARE LEXICON AND QUOTATION DICTIONARY, Alexander Schmidt. Full definitions, locations, shades of meaning in every word in plays and poems. More than 50,000 exact quotations. 1,485pp. 6½ × 9¼. 2-vol. set.
Vol. I: 22726-X Pa. $16.95
Vol. 2: 22727-8 Pa. $15.95

SELECTED POEMS, Emily Dickinson. Over 100 best-known, best-loved poems by one of America's foremost poets, reprinted from authoritative early editions. No comparable edition at this price. Index of first lines. 64pp. 5³⁄₁₆ × 8¼.
26466-1 Pa. $1.00

CELEBRATED CASES OF JUDGE DEE (DEE GOONG AN), translated by Robert van Gulik. Authentic 18th-century Chinese detective novel; Dee and associates solve three interlocked cases. Led to van Gulik's own stories with same characters. Extensive introduction. 9 illustrations. 237pp. 5⅜ × 8½.
23337-5 Pa. $6.95

THE MALLEUS MALEFICARUM OF KRAMER AND SPRENGER, translated by Montague Summers. Full text of most important witchhunter's "bible," used by both Catholics and Protestants. 278pp. 6⅝ × 10. 22802-9 Pa. $11.95

SPANISH STORIES/CUENTOS ESPAÑOLES: A Dual-Language Book, Angel Flores (ed.). Unique format offers 13 great stories in Spanish by Cervantes, Borges, others. Faithful English translations on facing pages. 352pp. 5⅜ × 8½.
25399-6 Pa. $8.95

THE CHICAGO WORLD'S FAIR OF 1893: A Photographic Record, Stanley Appelbaum (ed.). 128 rare photos show 200 buildings, Beaux-Arts architecture, Midway, original Ferris Wheel, Edison's kinetoscope, more. Architectural emphasis; full text. 116pp. 8¼ × 11. 23990-X Pa. $9.95

OLD QUEENS, N.Y., IN EARLY PHOTOGRAPHS, Vincent F. Seyfried and William Asadorian. Over 160 rare photographs of Maspeth, Jamaica, Jackson Heights, and other areas. Vintage views of DeWitt Clinton mansion, 1939 World's Fair and more. Captions. 192pp. 8⅞ × 11. 26358-4 Pa. $12.95

CAPTURED BY THE INDIANS: 15 Firsthand Accounts, 1750–1870, Frederick Drimmer. Astounding true historical accounts of grisly torture, bloody conflicts, relentless pursuits, miraculous escapes and more, by people who lived to tell the tale. 384pp. 5⅜ × 8½. 24901-8 Pa. $8.95

THE WORLD'S GREAT SPEECHES, Lewis Copeland and Lawrence W. Lamm (eds.). Vast collection of 278 speeches of Greeks to 1970. Powerful and effective models; unique look at history. 842pp. 5⅜ × 8½. 20468-5 Pa. $14.95

THE BOOK OF THE SWORD, Sir Richard F. Burton. Great Victorian scholar/adventurer's eloquent, erudite history of the "queen of weapons"—from prehistory to early Roman Empire. Evolution and development of early swords, variations (sabre, broadsword, cutlass, scimitar, etc.), much more. 336pp. 6⅛ × 9¼. 25434-8 Pa. $8.95

AUTOBIOGRAPHY: The Story of My Experiments with Truth, Mohandas K. Gandhi. Boyhood, legal studies, purification, the growth of the Satyagraha (nonviolent protest) movement. Critical, inspiring work of the man responsible for the freedom of India. 480pp. 5⅜ × 8½. (USO) 24593-4 Pa. $8.95

CELTIC MYTHS AND LEGENDS, T. W. Rolleston. Masterful retelling of Irish and Welsh stories and tales. Cuchulain, King Arthur, Deirdre, the Grail, many more. First paperback edition. 58 full-page illustrations. 512pp. 5⅜ × 8½. 26507-2 Pa. $9.95

THE PRINCIPLES OF PSYCHOLOGY, William James. Famous long course complete, unabridged. Stream of thought, time perception, memory, experimental methods; great work decades ahead of its time. 94 figures. 1,391pp. 5⅜ × 8½. 2-vol. set.
Vol. I: 20381-6 Pa. $12.95
Vol. II: 20382-4 Pa. $12.95

THE WORLD AS WILL AND REPRESENTATION, Arthur Schopenhauer. Definitive English translation of Schopenhauer's life work, correcting more than 1,000 errors, omissions in earlier translations. Translated by E. F. J. Payne. Total of 1,269pp. 5⅜ × 8½. 2-vol. set.
Vol. 1: 21761-2 Pa. $11.95
Vol. 2: 21762-0 Pa. $11.95

MAGIC AND MYSTERY IN TIBET, Madame Alexandra David-Neel. Experiences among lamas, magicians, sages, sorcerers, Bonpa wizards. A true psychic discovery. 32 illustrations. 321pp. 5⅜ × 8½. (USO) 22682-4 Pa. $8.95

THE EGYPTIAN BOOK OF THE DEAD, E. A. Wallis Budge. Complete reproduction of Ani's papyrus, finest ever found. Full hieroglyphic text, interlinear transliteration, word-for-word translation, smooth translation. 533pp. 6½ × 9¼. 21866-X Pa. $9.95

MATHEMATICS FOR THE NONMATHEMATICIAN, Morris Kline. Detailed, college-level treatment of mathematics in cultural and historical context, with numerous exercises. Recommended Reading Lists. Tables. Numerous figures. 641pp. 5⅜ × 8½. 24823-2 Pa. $11.95

THEORY OF WING SECTIONS: Including a Summary of Airfoil Data, Ira H. Abbott and A. E. von Doenhoff. Concise compilation of subsonic aerodynamic characteristics of NACA wing sections, plus description of theory. 350pp. of tables. 693pp. 5⅜ × 8½. 60586-8 Pa. $14.95

THE RIME OF THE ANCIENT MARINER, Gustave Doré, S. T. Coleridge. Doré's finest work; 34 plates capture moods, subtleties of poem. Flawless full-size reproductions printed on facing pages with authoritative text of poem. "Beautiful. Simply beautiful."—Publisher's Weekly. 77pp. 9¼ × 12. 22305-1 Pa. $6.95

NORTH AMERICAN INDIAN DESIGNS FOR ARTISTS AND CRAFTS-PEOPLE, Eva Wilson. Over 360 authentic copyright-free designs adapted from Navajo blankets, Hopi pottery, Sioux buffalo hides, more. Geometrics, symbolic figures, plant and animal motifs, etc. 128pp. 8⅜ × 11. (EUK) 25341-4 Pa. $7.95

SCULPTURE: Principles and Practice, Louis Slobodkin. Step-by-step approach to clay, plaster, metals, stone; classical and modern. 253 drawings, photos. 255pp. 8⅛ × 11. 22960-2 Pa. $10.95

CATALOG OF DOVER BOOKS

THE INFLUENCE OF SEA POWER UPON HISTORY, 1660-1783, A. T. Mahan. Influential classic of naval history and tactics still used as text in war colleges. First paperback edition. 4 maps. 24 battle plans. 640pp. 5⅜ × 8½.
25509-3 Pa. $12.95

THE STORY OF THE TITANIC AS TOLD BY ITS SURVIVORS, Jack Winocour (ed.). What it was really like. Panic, despair, shocking inefficiency, and a little heroism. More thrilling than any fictional account. 26 illustrations. 320pp. 5⅜ × 8½. 20610-6 Pa. $8.95

FAIRY AND FOLK TALES OF THE IRISH PEASANTRY, William Butler Yeats (ed.). Treasury of 64 tales from the twilight world of Celtic myth and legend: "The Soul Cages," "The Kildare Pooka," "King O'Toole and his Goose," many more. Introduction and Notes by W. B. Yeats. 352pp. 5⅜ × 8½. 26941-8 Pa. $8.95

BUDDHIST MAHAYANA TEXTS, E. B. Cowell and Others (eds.). Superb, accurate translations of basic documents in Mahayana Buddhism, highly important in history of religions. The Buddha-karita of Asvaghosha, Larger Sukhavativyuha, more. 448pp. 5⅜ × 8½. 25552-2 Pa. $9.95

ONE TWO THREE . . . INFINITY: Facts and Speculations of Science, George Gamow. Great physicist's fascinating, readable overview of contemporary science: number theory, relativity, fourth dimension, entropy, genes, atomic structure, much more. 128 illustrations. Index. 352pp. 5⅜ × 8½. 25664-2 Pa. $8.95

ENGINEERING IN HISTORY, Richard Shelton Kirby, et al. Broad, nontechnical survey of history's major technological advances: birth of Greek science, industrial revolution, electricity and applied science, 20th-century automation, much more. 181 illustrations. ". . . excellent . . ."—Isis. Bibliography. vii + 530pp. 5⅜ × 8¼.
26412-2 Pa. $14.95

Prices subject to change without notice.

Available at your book dealer or write for free catalog to Dept. GI, Dover Publications, Inc., 31 East 2nd St., Mineola, N.Y. 11501. Dover publishes more than 500 books each year on science, elementary and advanced mathematics, biology, music, art, literary history, social sciences and other areas.